7/00

THE PROCRASTINATOR'S GUIDE TO SUCCESS

Lynn Lively

D1125738

McGraw-Hill

New York   San Francisco   Washington, D.C.   Auckland   Bogotá
Caracas   Lisbon   London   Madrid   Mexico City   Milan
Montreal   New Delhi   San Juan   Singapore
Sydney   Tokyo   Toronto

Library of Congress Cataloging-in-Publication Data

Lively, Lynn.
    The procrastinator's guide to success / Lynn Lively.
       p.   cm.
    ISBN 0-07-038307-3 (alk. paper)
    1. Success—Psychological aspects. 2. Procrastination.
  I. Title.
  BF637.S8L55 1999
  155.2'32–dc21   99-14473
                                           CIP

McGraw-Hill

*A Division of The **McGraw·Hill** Companies*

2 3 4 5 6 7 8 9 0 DOC / DOC 9 0 9 8 7 6 5 4 3 2 1 0 9

ISBN 0-07-038307-3

Printed and bound by R.R. Donnelley & Sons Company.

 This book is printed on recycled, acid-free paper
containing a minimum of 50% recycled de-inked fiber.

McGraw-Hill books are available at special quantity discounts to
use as premiums and sales promotions, or for use in corporate
training programs. For more information, please write to the
Director of Special Sales, McGraw-Hill, 11 West 19th Street, New
York, NY 10011. Or contact your local bookstore.

To Nathan

CONTENTS

Procrastinate No More   17

This chapter contains an assortment of ways you can pro-crastinate less. Have fun with it. No single technique works for every situation. Mix and match, use and discard, and add your own personal stamp.

Why Do You Procrastinate?   37

Let's take a look at why you procrastinate. You are not a bad person, lazy, or incompetent. You are human. Once you figure out what you are doing to yourself, you can get yourself mov-ing again.

Success Means Entering the Risk Zone   57

Once you stop procrastinating and do something, you enter the Risk Zone. You might fail, lose, or be wrong, but entering the Risk Zone means you might also succeed, win, and be right. If you don't try, you know what the outcome will be. But if you give it your best shot, the possibilities are endless. Let's take a look at risk.

5 Overcoming Inertia: A BEGIN-er's Checklist

No, not a beginner in the sense of never having done something before. This is a BEGIN-er's checklist, because you are ready to begin, right? Use this list when you are still stuck to help you identify what is stopping you and what to do about it.

PART II. RESOLUTION

You like yourself and your life better perhaps because you've made progress on your to-do list, applied for that new opportunity, or cleared up the conflict with your coworker that has been worrying you. Now it's time to go to the next level, to think more clearly, to make real strides toward lifelong

CONTENTS

progress. You're ready to become more decisive, to become a resolver! Follow this guide to make decisions that are important, are long term, or are worrying you.

R E S O L V E IT!

6

R: Resolve Something!

You can't do it all, so where are you going to begin? This chapter will help you set priorities and decide what to do first. You will use a series of sorts to bring order to the chaos that is whirling around in your mind. After you finish your sorts, you will feel tension and anxiety ebb away. Get started; peace of mind awaits you!

7

E: Examine What You Already Know

Information is the raw material of every decision, and this chapter shows you how to figure out what you already know and use it to your advantage. History is unlikely to repeat itself, but you certainly can learn from the past. Doing so will keep you from making mistakes in the future.

S: Step into the Future   149

You will be far more successful if you envision where you want to go instead of drifting or doing what's easy. By following a few simple steps, you can anticipate the impact on tomorrow of what you are doing today. This chapter shows you a step-by-step process for building the future you want for yourself.

O: Overcome the Subtle Factors   171

The mark of a good decision maker is picking up on cues that other people miss. This chapter shows you how to go beyond the obvious—such as budget projections and computer reports—and master the subtle. That ability can make you or break you!

CONTENTS

12

E: Enjoy Your Success or Learn from Experience and Then Move On   235

If things have turned out well, consciously enjoy your success. You've earned it. If you are not so satisfied, lick your wounds, learn what you can, and seek perspective. Both success and failure are temporary conditions. Life is moving on, and so are you.

13

Afterword   245

Once you stop procrastinating and start resolving issues, prepare for your life to change. You will face choices and opportunities you never imagined. You will be a role model for others and a contributor to a better society. Exciting times lie ahead. What are you going to do? Now you know.

Index   251

PREFACE

as this ever happened to you?

December 1 was the day I was going to start this book, and it began well. The alarm buzzed at 6:45 a.m., and by 7:00 I was back in bed reading the morning paper with my cat on my lap. I leisurely sipped a cup of decaf tea with just a hint of Lapsang souchong added for flavor. Promptly at 7:45 I got dressed and began my "maintenance hour" at 8 a.m. sharp. (I have learned that my brain doesn't become fully active until 9 a.m., so scheduling an hour in which I concentrate on personal-household-professional "maintenance items"—for example, arranging repairs, calling friends, and following up on things in general—works well for me.) At 9:00 I had just a *few* more essential calls to make, so I kept going. I moved this year's IRA to a mutual fund, a task that had been on my to-do list for 11 months now; scheduled repair of my roof, which had been leaking for over 6 months; and called a friend to see what her Christmas plans were. It wasn't until 10:30, when I hung up after telephoning a Mountaineers Club acquaintance to tell her that I would *not* be signing up for her hike, that I started laughing at myself.

PREFACE

What a great start for a book on procrastination, I reflected with amusement. For procrastination it was; there was no other word to describe what I had been doing. In addition to catching myself (and not kidding myself about how I was spending my time), I spent my lunch hour moving all my personal maintenance items out of my office, removing one source of temptation and distraction. I also dumped a giant pile of articles I had been meaning to skim on my conference-work table so that there was no doubt in my mind what the best use of my time was and turned my telephone ringer to "off." In short, I got myself back on track.

And that's what I want you to do too: learn tips, techniques, and guidelines you can use to get yourself back on track, moving steadily toward your goal. Right now give up any fantasy that you will stop procrastinating—because you never will. The temptation will always be there. But you can procrastinate less, and you can procrastinate strategically—when it makes sense for you. You can learn to catch yourself sooner, apply tricks to help you focus, create a sense of direction for what to do next, and develop the resolve to do it.

This book will offer you ways to overcome procrastination. Note that I didn't say "the way." That's because you are going to use this information to develop "your way," a way that works for you. You are going to build on your talents and strengths to do more of what works and less of what doesn't. You are going to succeed on your terms. But this book is more; it is also a framework for making decisions when you don't know what to do. It will show you how to move beyond procrastination to resolution, how to create practical (not perfect) solutions to complicated situations.

If you know what to do, Part I shows you how to overcome procrastination and take action, uncover a direction to take, and begin that fascinating project you have always wanted to do. This section also shows you how to finish what is undone. Just think how interesting your world will become as you open new doors for yourself and create a life that is full of variety, challenge, and accomplishment. You can savor an hour of joy each day—a time just for you. Imagine how much mental energy you will free up as you let go of those nagging worries. Pause for a moment and think. Do you want to begin something new, end something that's over, or let go of what's been hanging around too long?

If you don't know what to do, Part II is even more exciting because here you promote yourself from procrastinator to resolver. "Resolver" is a mind-set that describes you as you resolve situations. You decide what you are going to do, and you do it. You are a procrastinator no more. This concept is astounding. Just think— as your life unfolds, you will greet each day with enthusiasm because you are no longer afraid. You know that no matter what twists and turns your path in life takes, you will savor the opportunities, cope with the tragedies and disappointments, and move on to the next unfolding event.

Success is a very personal thing. Simply put, it's a state of mind; it's whatever you decide it is for you. But it's more. Success is also an action mode; success means you make things happen. Procrastination—the failure to make things happen—is a major barrier to living an interesting life, a barrier this book will help you overcome. Turn the page to Chapter 1 and let's get started *now*!

What am I going
to do about...?

I really must talk
to her soon...

**What clouds of unfinished business
are hanging around your mind,
your day, your life?**

You know you need to "do something."
But instead you procrastinate. You worry
endlessly and talk (and talk) about what
you're going to do, while you feel your life
slipping away like sand through an hourglass.

STOP! It's time for a new approach. Take a
deep breath right now and concentrate.
Picture your situation in your mind.
Now, ask yourself:

Do *you* know what to do?

I need to get started
on that report...

I promised him I
would fix that...

Yes

If your answer is yes, you know what
to do and aren't doing it ———

*Go to Part I for tips and techniques
on how to overcome procrastination*

No

If your answer is no, you don't
know what to do, then you are not
procrastinating———

*Go to Part II for a framework for
making decisions.*

Chase those dreary old clouds away and expand your horizons!

When you overcome procrastination, life is interesting because you bring closure to all that
unfinished business and you move on. If you procrastinate today, the same tasks, worries,
and decisions will still be looming over you tomorrow. Instead, take action and move on;
seek new summits and adventures.

What are *you* going to do? The time to do something is now.

PART I
PROCRASTINATION

1 ARE YOU A PROCRASTINATOR?

O f course you are.

Everyone is, sometimes. Procrastination is a very human quality. But sheepishly admitting this fact is not going to move you forward to bring the closure and resolution you seek.

I believe the question is not, Are you a procrastinator? It is, What are you going to do about it, about the situation that caused you to pick up this book? You know what I'm talking about; perhaps it's the phone call you dread making, the investment you're afraid to buy, or the project you haven't begun. You have some unfinished business, and you would like to cross it off your to-do list and move on. I agree with you. It's time to do something, that is, to teach yourself to procrastinate less. After all, this is the rest of your life we're talking about, and the time to begin living it to the fullest is now.

> **Tip**
> *Who has high expectations for you? Call that person now to arrange a visit for coffee or lunch. And who can you inspire or encourage?*

The Procrastinator's Guide to Success is a book about *you*, about how you can overcome procrastination and savor each day. It tells

Confessions of a procrastinator

I lived seven years of my life—in my twenties—without any joy because I hadn't finished my master's thesis. There was no good reason. I simply moved from the university town before it was written, and my discipline faded. But not the guilt and self-hatred and sense of personal failure. It was a horrible time. I didn't read a book for seven years because I always "should" have been working on the paper. I viewed it like an invisible albatross, always hanging around my neck.

I wish I could tell you I cured myself, but I didn't. Instead I got a job where my boss sent out a press release announcing proudly to the world that "Lynn Lively, MA, has recently been appointed to the position of _____." My face turned ashen when I saw this document. "But Chris, I told you my degree has not been awarded. I don't have an MA yet." He smiled sweetly, but there was steel in his eyes when he said, "You also told me in the job interview you had your paper nearly done. I expect you to finish that degree."

So finish I did. I first petitioned the university for an extension and then wrote every evening after work for six weeks. I flew back to Ohio for an oral exam and on the way home had the joy of reading my first book for pleasure. And I vowed never to let procrastination wreck my life again.

The next time I was in graduate school, I decided to create a reward and set a firm deadline for myself. I scheduled a trip to Europe immediately after the final quarter ended. I ignored my whining that "I am not a morning person" and got myself up at 6 a.m. every morning and wrote and wrote. Europe was wonderful, and my paper was good enough to get a degree. And to this day I thank Chris for his high expectations.

you how you can experience the satisfaction that comes from a job well done, a disappointment faced and then shrugged off, an unpleasant conversation closed. It's a book about how you can create a daily "hour of joy" to do what you want, including the pleasure of doing nothing at all. It's about how you can make the rest of today, this week, and the rest of your life incredibly interesting and fulfilling.

This is not a book about how to live happily ever after, have it easy, or find someone else to tell you what to do. My approach presumes that you are ready, willing, and able to take responsibility for yourself and your decisions. But if you're seeking shortcuts, tips, and a sense of direction, reading this book will be an excellent investment in yourself. Every technique and system is one that you are perfectly able to do. And these ideas work.

I know because I—a very ordinary person, as you will see— have done them all myself. In addition, over the last 18 years I have also seen coworkers in my family-owned business master these techniques to become increasingly competent individuals. From the newest assembler to the most experienced general manager, people are able to operate independently and run our company during my frequent absences. Plus, as a professional speaker, writer, and consultant for the last 10 years, I have tested these ideas on thousands of people. These suggestions are a result of many years of refinement.

KEY QUESTION: DO YOU KNOW WHAT TO DO? YES OR NO

Have you considered the possibility that you are *not* a procrastinator?

I want you to ask yourself a question: Are you procrastinating because you know what to do and aren't doing it? Or are you "procrastinating" because you don't know what to do? Your answer is crucial because it determines what you will do next.

If you answer yes, you know what to do but are not doing it, you are a procrastinator. This is good news, because you only have one challenge: to get yourself to take action. Chapter 2 will give you lots of tips on how to do just that.

But if upon reflection you realize your answer is no, you don't know what to do, you are not a procrastinator. You are *thinking* about your situation, still trying to decide what to do. And that is a very different set of circumstances.

The reason you haven't taken action is because the action you should take isn't clear to you. And guess what: Even if you "do something," what are the odds you will do the right thing? Determinedly doing "something," "anything" is a recipe for having to do things over because of poor results or because you are not satisfied with your choice. Your initial challenge is to figure out what to do to resolve your situation, and Part II will show you just how to do that.

Tip
The proactive approach is a popular concept that can be misused. Granted, you appear very busy and productive to the world when you "do something, do anything." But if what you do doesn't move your life forward, you're wasting your time and resources. Don't let this buzzword influence you to move before you are ready.

WHAT PROCRASTINATION IS

It's time for definitions.

Procrastination: You know what to do, but you don't do it. *Thinking:* You don't know what to do. The two conditions are very different. Don't confuse them.

At its most elemental, procrastination is the failure to take action, to make something happen. You know what to do, but you don't do it. Solving this problem requires two things: First you need tips and techniques to nudge yourself forward, but in addition, you need to figure out *why* you are procrastinating. After all, you are a very intelligent person and can see the consequences of what you are doing. Procrastination is a condition that you often want to overcome or certainly do less often.

Thinking is the process of figuring out what to do. Thinking takes time and effort. It requires you to construct possibilities in your mind about outcomes that haven't happened yet. It is abstract. But it is an essential quality for success. Picture your future: As you become a better thinker, you will be caught less often by surprise, will be more able to get the results you want, and ultimately will cease to be afraid of change. You will know that you have the skills to cope with whatever happens to you as your career and life unfold.

Thinking as an activity is not well respected in our society. For one thing, when you are thinking, you appear to be "doing nothing." You could be sitting at your desk writing a grocery list, but to the casual passerby (make that boss?), you would appear more productive than if you were staring out the window considering your options and mulling over possibilities.

Thinking is some of the most fun you can have. We're talking about figuring out how you are going to live the rest of your life. What could possibly be more interesting? Thinking is like playing a game with stakes that really matter. Life is a puzzle, and the question is where you are going to move next. Sports scores pale in comparison to life scores! If you are still carrying around assumptions that thinking = school = tests, let them go.

Thinking = life skill = opportunities, personal growth, and interesting times.

Thinking is the basis of decisions, and decisions are what really matter, because they are the process by which you convert your thoughts to actions. If you don't know what to do, don't get discouraged. The tips in this book will help you.

> *Tip*
> *Whenever you are "caught" thinking, be sure to tell people that is what you are doing. Once they realize you are serious and hear your good ideas, they will be impressed.*

WHAT PROCRASTINATION IS NOT

Lots of things are called procrastination when they really aren't. There is no need to verbally abuse yourself over procrastinating just because you

- Choose to do nothing
- Take a nap
- Watch TV or a movie
- Go to lunch with a friend
- Clean a closet or file drawer
- Smell the roses and spring flowers

Unless you should be doing something else. And you know what that something else is. And you aren't doing it. Then you are a procrastinator.

All the wonderful things on the list above are just what you should be doing more of (if that list doesn't suit you, create your own). And you will, once you clean up all those guilty "shoulds" that make your conscience hurt.

> *Tip*
> *Challenge the "shoulds," those insidious guilt trips*
> *that drain your psychic energy. Don't let other peo-*
> *ple's expectations govern your life. Examine your*
> *own heart and mind to decide what you want to do,*
> *find necessary to do, or will no longer worry about.*

DON'T BEAT YOURSELF UP UNNECESSARILY

If you are procrastinating, say so. If you are not, don't use that word. Instead, say precisely what you are doing. As you refine your language, you probably will find that you are procrastinating far less often than you assumed.

For example, if you are procrastinating about making a phone call to tell a customer that a shipment has been delayed, your conversation with yourself might include something like: "Self, you are procrastinating on the Bethany Jones phone call. Bethany is probably going to yell when she finds out about the delay, but she's going to splutter even louder if she doesn't get a call until tomorrow. Pick up the phone and get it over with."

Conversely, if you realize that you are not procrastinating but instead are missing information, your talk with yourself might go something like this: "Self, Beth Jones is desperate to find out when that unit is going to arrive so she can let her customer know. I'd better check with shipping and find out when that delivery truck is going to be repaired so I can give her a realistic estimate."

> *Tip*
> *Using precise language will keep you focused about*
> *what to do next, provide useful information to others*
> *about what to expect, and keep you from under- or*
> *overexaggerating the amount of effort that remains.*

CHAPTER ONE

YOUR GOAL: AN HOUR OF JOY PER DAY

Just think how pleasant your life will be once you learn how to overcome procrastination, the big, bad P. You will create the time to do what you want. Even better, you will be rid of the nagging guilt that may keep you from enjoying what you want—nay, deserve—to do! I am firmly convinced that finally finishing that task that is nagging at you will free up more than time. It will free up your spirit.

Stop right now and visualize what you would do with an extra gift of time today. Let those positive possibilities entice you beyond the guilty "shoulds."

> **Tip**
> *It's rarely too late to complete unfinished business. However, it may no longer be worth your effort. Ask yourself whether your life will be more interesting with closure or with letting go of the "shoulds." Then proceed accordingly.*

SIGNS OF PROCRASTINATION

An important step to overcoming procrastination is to admit you have a problem. Procrastination is not a personality defect; it is a condition to be remedied. Here is a simple checklist to help you recognize the signs of procrastination.

You are procrastinating when you

Simply can't face making a phone call

Hate the thought of making someone unhappy

Dread the flak you are going to get

Never get around to doing what you want to do because of that great big "should" looming over you

Watch *Seinfeld* reruns but don't enjoy them

Eat too many cookies, and

(Add your personal foibles here)

Note that uncertainty about what to do is not part of this list. You know exactly what to do; you simply aren't doing it. You, my friend, are a procrastinator.

Recognizing these or similar symptoms should cause you great joy. Every one of these conditions can be remedied, and quickly. It's when you don't know what to do that things become complicated.

SIGNS OF THINKING

Often people confuse what they ought to do with knowing precisely what to do and how to do it. Here is a checklist to help you confirm that you are still mulling over your options.

You are thinking when you

Change your mind frequently

Feel uncertain, confused, and overwhelmed

Sense that your "homework" isn't done

Can't decide what to do

Should get started but aren't organized yet

Are not ready to begin

Are in limbo

Don't know precisely where to start or whom to call

(Add your personal mind-set here)

Take comfort if these mental descriptions apply to you. You are not crazy, dumb, or lazy. You also are not a procrastinator. You are a person who is thinking, considering options, and getting ready to make the best decision possible. You will soon learn how to RESOLVE It!

Confessions of a procrastinator

Nathan thought he was a procrastinator because his sales brochure was way behind schedule. He was embarrassed working trade shows with a color photocopy. One day a talented graphic artist made a cold call looking for contract work and lucked out when on impulse Nathan said yes, he thought her skills might be just what he needed to help him finish the project quickly. She appeared at the office an hour later and Nathan showed her to a marketing table littered with photographs, text fragments, and old brochures. At the end of the day they both sadly concluded that Nathan was not ready to delegate this project. New photography was needed, the product mix wasn't firm, and the text was so technical that only Nathan could draft it. This was not a case of procrastination; this was the creative process of a preparing a brochure. Luckily, the inaccurate perception cost each of them only a day of work.

Tip
If something is not easy to finish, you probably are not procrastinating. Suspect that you are thinking and give yourself credit for slogging your way through a complicated job.

PROCRASTINATE PROPERLY

If you haven't figured it out by now, I believe that *procrastination* is a neutral term that defines a situation in which you want to challenge yourself to take an action. In fact, sometimes procrastination can be a good thing. What you want to do is procrastinate strategically, that is, consciously delay taking action when it benefits you to do so. Here is a list of pros and the cons to get you thinking about when procrastination makes sense.

THE PROS OF PROCRASTINATION

By all means procrastinate if it will help you

Create time for something else that is more important

Put a trivial issue into perspective

Cool down your anger

Get more useful information

See if an issue will go away on its own

Survive an "off day" when you are mentally frazzled

Realize that your issue is a "should" and not anything you want and/or need to finish

Maintain the status quo, which is good enough

Lower the stress on you and others

Pause before snapping at a friend

Reduce the odds that you will have to redo, start over, fix, correct, or rewrite

Give you more time to convince your boss or coworkers of your position

(Add your own benefits here)

THE CONS OF PROCRASTINATION

Do *not* procrastinate if doing so will cause you to

Be perceived as lazy, incompetent, or indecisive

Drain your mental energy

Miss an opportunity

Bore your friends with your repetitive excuses

Bore yourself with your endless moaning and self-loathing

Not get credit for a good idea

Make a situation worse (especially one involving money or people)

Lose preparation time by getting a late start

Delay your coworkers or cause them problems

Reduce the amount of time available for a correction or rework

Lose your competitive edge in the marketplace

Cause you to be perceived as part of the problem rather than part of the solution

(Add your own risks here)

Review both of these lists and compare them to your situation. Ask yourself whether procrastinating is doing you more good or harm. Then take the next step accordingly.

> **Tip**
> Describe your situation using neutral, accurate language. For example, replace "I hate myself for not starting that project" with "My project is due in three weeks. Do I know exactly where to start?" Doing so will enable you to think more clearly about the best thing to do next.

LYNN'S LAWS FOR SUCCESS

Throughout this book you will find three key underlying assumptions which I want to present now. They govern my life and thus these pages. By bringing them to your conscious level, I hope you will use them to challenge your own thinking and decision making so that you can live the most interesting life possible.

Law 1: You always have a choice, and that choice is to do something or do nothing.

To do something is to be proactive, to take charge of your life. Does that make sense for you right now? This book has a very strong bias toward action, but there are exceptions. For example, if you have recently experienced hard times, maybe you just need to drift for a bit. Conversely, when you are procrastinating, you are choosing—consciously or unconsciously—to do nothing. Is that the way you want to live? Life is a combination of choosing to do something and choosing to do nothing. Make your choices consciously.

Law 2: Do things right and you will not have to do so many things over.

An activity half done or poorly done rarely brings satisfaction or good results. Constantly challenge yourself to let go of what you don't really care about and concentrate on what brings you joy or a reward. Investing your time up front in thinking and planning will create more time for you later because the task or job has been done and done right. You can move on to something new with enthusiasm.

Law 3: Your decisions are the building blocks of your life, and your mind is your most valuable decision-making tool.

Every choice you make today is creating your tomorrow. Most decisions are trivial, but not all. The trick is to know the difference and put your energy where the payoff is greatest. And treasure your mind, for that's where you spend all your time. Why not make a few improvements? After all, it's paid for, well educated, and far more powerful than your computer, and nobody else has one quite like it. Learning how to better tap its abilities is one of the best investments in yourself you can make.

Remember

Everyone procrastinates. The question is, is doing nothing working for you or against you? If you are going to procrastinate, do it strategically.

Ask yourself whether you know what to do about your situation. If so, you are procrastinating. If you don't know what to do, you are thinking. The two conditions are different. Your personal and professional success requires a combination of both approaches.

Enough philosophy. It's time to overcome procrastination. Turn to Chapter 2 for tips, techniques, and tricks.

2 PROCRASTINATE NO MORE

The recipe for successfully overcoming procrastination has two ingredients: external behaviors and internal processes. First, you want to modify your behavior by punching through the inactivity that has you paralyzed. The other half of the equation—why you procrastinate and what's going on in your head, including the emotional aspects—will be covered in later chapters.

Your first challenge is to create a model of success for yourself. You want to define yourself differently. This chapter presents a list of things you can do to get yourself started, immediate actions you can take that will help you overcome procrastination. Here you concentrate on the quick fix, the jump start, and things that don't require a lot of time or money.

SUCCESS: PROCRASTINATION AS A NONISSUE

Your goal is to make procrastination a nonissue for most of your waking hours. *Nonissue* is one of my favorite terms. It's self-descriptive: a condition that doesn't exist. Nonissues totally eliminate judgment: deciding whether something is good or bad. And when you eliminate judgment, tremendous emotional energy is freed. Sure, you're human and occasionally slip, but generally you define yourself as a capable individual who is clearly focused, does what's important, and savors at least one hour of joy each day. Even if you used to procrastinate, so what? That was a long time ago—like yesterday.

You'll know you've succeeded when the subject of procrastination comes up and you are taken aback. You look blankly at your conversational partners and say, "Gee, I don't think about procrastination very much. I just do what I have defined as important to me." Then, of course, you may give them copies of this book on their next birthdays.

Note: Do not play on false modesty and demur that of course you struggle when you actually don't. You will do your friends a far bigger favor by offering them a role model and hope for getting their own lives under control. Be proud of what you have accomplished. Your life is interesting and not unduly frazzled, and you made it happen. Yay for you!

Confessions of a procrastinator

Sang wanted to stop smoking but kept putting it off. He was discouraged because none of his previous efforts had been successful for more than a few days. Then came the wake-up call, literally. His mother telephoned sobbing to tell him his father had just been diagnosed with lung cancer.

Sang realized this was it. He was scared, he had a family history, and the time to quit was now. That night he went home to his apartment and very matter-of-factly threw away the ashtrays, matches, and remaining cigarettes. Over the next week he laundered his curtains and blankets to get rid of all smoke smells. He put up a no-smoking sign at his front door. He bought hard candy to keep his ner-

(cont.)

vous hands busy. But the most powerful thing he did was undergo a mind shift: Beginning with his mother's phone call, he defined himself as a non-smoker. Thus, when friends would offer him a cigarette, he replied, "No thanks, I don't smoke." He never brought the subject up himself, and when friends asked him what was going on and tried to make a big deal of this change, he appeared bored. This was old history; he simply was a nonsmoker now. He let go of the few friends who wouldn't respect his new status and found different activities, especially ones that kept his hands busy.

That was 20 years ago, and Sang has never wavered. When asked, he still says his secret to quitting smoking was the mind shift to nonsmoker.

Question: Do you need a mind shift?

SUCCESS IS SELF-VALIDATING: CREATE SUCCESS AS OFTEN AS YOU CAN

Try some of these tips or try them all. Promise yourself you won't conclude that something doesn't work until you have tried it at least once. Do not permit yourself to dismiss these ideas with a disdainful "I already knew that." You may know them, but are you doing them? Action is the mark of a nonprocrastinator; you no longer talk about why something won't work but instead concentrate on how you can make something work for you. Have fun with these suggestions; refine them, improve them, and let them inspire you.

One caveat: Procrastination is a complex human behavior for which there is no permanent cure. For better or worse, it's a part of you that usually is under control but sometimes is not. So don't be discouraged if you are disciplined one day and a sloth the next. Life is like that. Call it the need for "continuous improvement" if that makes you feel better.

As you read these pages, look for things you already do—and need to do more often; things you have forgotten to try in a while—and might try again, new ideas that appeal to you in terms of your personal style, and things that didn't work for you in the past but might with a minor tweak. Every individual is different. Your goal is to do more of what works and less of what doesn't.

The tips are grouped into three different types of approaches, including things to start, things to stop, and fresh approaches.

Things to Start

The following are suggestions for things to start, to do more of. These action items provide an enormous return on investment. Try them; they work!

Figure out what has the biggest payoff and do that first. This is my absolute favorite. You have a finite number of minutes each day, the same as everybody else. How do you want to spend them? The trick is to be candid with yourself about what the payoff is for you and not to let those "shoulds" take over. Another way of saying this is to focus on what you decide is important and invest in yourself. If you're in doubt, review the duties in your job description or mission statement. Have you drifted?

How? Rank-order your choices by importance of outcome. Then concentrate your energy on what matters and let go of the rest. Conduct an annual self-assessment of yourself, your values, and how they are reflected in your personal and professional life. Label a steno pad "Life Notebook" and every New Year's Day leave the football game to sit down with a cup of tea and update it. Draw a picture of your life in balance, assigning time to mental, physical, spiritual, and emotional efforts.

Confessions of a procrastinator

Suzanne and Chikara wanted to move to a sunnier climate, but they were stuck. He was a 55-year-old general surgeon who preferred medicine to running a business. Starting a practice in a new state would be next to impossible because the licensing requirements and medical exams were designed for people just out of residency. Also, he was a naturalized American and all his school records were in Japan. The two thought their fate was sealed. Before giving up, they decided to take a new approach. They sat down one day and challenged themselves to brainstorm options. They came up with seeing the world by joining the military. Would the army, navy, air force or marines be interested in a very "experienced" doctor? There was only one way to find out, and that was to apply.

The process took them two years of filling out applications, requesting records from overseas, and overcoming objections. Then Chikara's navy physical uncovered Type II, non-insulin-dependent adult-onset diabetes that had to be brought under control. But they never gave up. And five days short of Chikara's 57th birthday, the absolute last day for induction, he was proudly sworn in as a commander, U.S. Navy, with Suzanne by his side. They sold their practice and their big house and first moved to Oakland, and then a year later to Japan for a tour of duty. For his final tour they anticipate Hawaii. Chikara and Suzanne are heroes to me because they made their dreams come true.

Ask yourself: A year from now, will what I am doing (or not doing) right now help me, hurt me, or be a nonissue?

Tip

Reorder your to-do list. Put your big-payoff items at the top and cross off low-return priorities. You can't do it all, so do what counts.

Tip

The thought of big projects is exhausting, so you procrastinate. Break them into small parts and do one of those parts today.

Create confidence builders. Identify something you *can* do and make that where you begin. Success is the result of doing many small things and doing enough of them right that you keep making steady forward progress. Vow that no matter how busy your day is and how many interruptions you encounter, you will do *one* thing to move you toward your goal. Doing even one thing often breaks the log jam of inertia.

How? Create a list on which the first item is incredibly simple and very specific. A telephone call is a good place to start. Things you might include in your list are: finding the Yellow Pages and putting it on your desk—you could even paper clip the pages where you will begin your research; looking up a telephone number in your database and writing it on scrap paper, along with your question; leaving a voice mail even though an office is closed; and figuring out the time zone of an area code so you can pick a time to make a call. Try this tip for sure. I find that making just one phone call is one of the most powerful tricks you can play on myself.

Ask yourself: Can I get on the telephone and find out a price, make an appointment, ask for a referral, get product details, set a date, or request information?

Tip

Start your project in an unusual place. Make that first phone call while waiting at the airport, in a restaurant, or at a colleague's office. Pluck a catalog from that pile to be studied and put it in your briefcase now. Then place an order or ask some questions the next time you have a few spare moments. Make steady progress by effectively using little "niblets" of time. And congratulate yourself for your discipline when you realize you are not one of those people who wastes time and looks bored.

Start complex tasks when fresh; complete easy jobs when tired. Most people have more energy in the morning after a night's rest, and that means mornings are probably the best time to start a job that requires thought. Therefore, prepare yourself the night before. That way, when you first walk into your office, you'll be better able to resist the temptation to pick up that less important item. If you are a slow starter, be firm with yourself, stating aloud, that "After I finish this cup of coffee, I will _____."

How? Separate your piles of work. For example, the last thing in the evening, put the report you are going to edit the next day smack in the middle of your desk with sharpened pencils laying alongside it. Then, on top of a bookcase or file cabinet, start a pile of less demanding work, such as third-class mail to read, computer leads to update, or in my case, chapters to proof and edit. For example, this chapter has been edited while I was waiting for my car to go through a car wash, in a travel clinic waiting for a hepatitis shot, and in line to pick up airplane tickets.

> **Tip**
> *Control interruptions. Just because someone else thinks his or her question is of vital importance, you don't have to agree. You are in charge of your time. If your boss is an interrupter, propose a meeting every two hours so that you can bring completed work to him or her.*

Be your own biggest fan.   Listen to your self-talk. Are you motivating and encouraging yourself? If not, it's time to start. It's easy to let your internal language deteriorate into that of a displeased parent scolding yourself. Once you're past 10, feeling like a naughty child is not likely to be motivating; all it does is make you more stubborn.

How? Give yourself a term of endearment and use it. Pick either an incredibly powerful term like "president of (your name) enterprises" or the fuzziest, silliest baby-talk name you can think of, like the one you use with your cat when she is being cute. Try something like: "Come on, you smart little snuffle bunny, pick up that phone. I know you can do it!" You can also use this label as a password on your voice mail or computer; you'll laugh every time.

Ask yourself: What term describes the self I want to be? Then use it a lot.

> **Tip**
> *Make new friends if your old ones don't like the new you. Seek out and spend time with people you admire. You're growing and evolving; so are your friendships.*

Start sooner.   This tip is for all you smart people who picked up bad habits in grade school. If you learned you could do your work the night before and still get A's, it's time to examine that behavior pattern. First, you're not in sixth grade anymore; your work is far more complex and requires more thought and effort than taking notes from the encyclopedia. Second, somebody is counting on you. The slower you are to start, the more you will stress your coworkers and cause them to have to rush. You are not a good team member, and you will be labeled as such. Finally, you're worrying yourself unnecessarily. It's time to grow up.

How? Set a finish date and then plan your time backward from then to today. Use more realistic time estimates. Budget time for delays, peer reviews, people out on vacation, your own mistakes, lost computer files, and so on. Starting sooner is a terrific way to reduce your stress level.

Ask yourself: Will waiting to start this task help me, my coworkers, or the quality of the finished product? If not, take a deep breath and begin.

Tip
Don't reward yourself for bad behavior. Consciously discipline yourself and take away a privilege when you catch yourself in a late start. Pretend you are your own mentor and coach yourself to do better.

Things to Stop

The following are suggestions for things to do less of. Redirecting your efforts will free up your time for more important tasks, help you reexamine any ruts you might be in, and force you to stop kidding yourself about where your energy is going.

Stop busywork. Activities that require effort but provide little reward are busywork. They are very dangerous because you feel productive but on reflection realize you have exerted tremendous energy and gotten very little reward. If your resources are limited and you are not doing the important things, question yourself and see if you need redirection.

How? Look for a long-term payoff. Spend your time preparing for the future. Be alert for activities that will cause you to spend energy on what already has been done. Avoid time wasters. Be honest with yourself and eliminate one today. For example, one thing that comes to mind is balancing a checkbook for the year already passed. Financial management is a very good use of your time, but if you are seriously behind in your reconciliation, the thing to do is to start with your next bank statement. Yes, banks can make mistakes; but they rarely do. And because the task of examining all those old statements is so daunting, you probably will never do it anyway. Go forward!

Here's a busywork alert list. Use it to challenge your thinking: weekly car wash, fancy file labels, daily bed making, daily grocery shopping, ironing, daily papers, weekly reports, partial loads of wash, frequent e-mail checks, meetings when you aren't on the agenda, gabbing in the halls, individual (rather than grouped) errands, routine maintenance, touch-up painting, individual rather than group updates, twenty-five-cents-off coupons, small quantities, TV news, fancy cooking, duplicate reports.

Ask yourself: Is my effort commensurate with my reward?

Tip
Propose to your boss or team that the (you name it) report be done half as often or not at all. Have a good reason for the reduction and entice them with the possibilities for what could be done instead. You'll be a hero.

Set aside hopelessness and other forms of negative thinking.
Indulging in feelings of pity, woe, and poor little me moaning are self-

indulgent luxuries that are not going to solve your problem. Plus, it gets boring for you and others. Some things just are, and you have to deal with them. Also, give up second-guessing yourself about the past; concentrate on the exciting life you are creating today.

How? Stand up, look straight ahead, and say very firmly out loud to yourself: "I am a very capable adult human who is now going to tap my many resources and face this problem. It is time for a fresh approach." Then literally turn 180 degrees in the other direction, pick up a pencil and paper, and start a list of what to do or whom to call for advice. Then do something.

Ask yourself: What can I do about this? Don't ask: Why did this happen to me?

Tip
Get a different haircut. Tell yourself it's the start of the new you, a nonprocrastinator.

Forgive previous mistakes and expect new ones.   Nobody is perfect, including you. Not only that, nobody but you cares that you aren't perfect. You have to try again. Lick your wounds and move on.

How? Take a piece of scrap paper and write down exactly what you did wrong and how stupid you felt and how embarrassed you were. Be as negative as you want; totally dump every piece of painful memory that you are carrying onto this paper. Then very thoroughly crumple up the paper and throw it away. And with it, throw away the necessity to ever bring it to your conscious level again. The incident is over, and you have moved on. *Note:* If you are paranoid about this paper being discovered, another option is to tear it into small bits, drive to a trash can at a city park, and discard it there. Then take a walk around the park.

Ask yourself: What painful reminder can I purge from my subconscious right now?

> *Tip*
> *Read a biography to gain perspective on the mis-*
> *takes others have made—and survived. Inspire*
> *yourself with the success of others. For example, I*
> *like to read about groundbreaking contemporary*
> *women such as Helen Gurley Brown, who wrote* Sex
> and the Single Girl *and* The Late Show. *Such role*
> *models remind me that these women took chances*
> *and survived and I can too.*

Curtail volunteer activities and hobbies.   Another activity to question is time spent on extracurricular activities. Would you be better off increasing professional skills that will give you a more interesting tomorrow? If you are doing the important things in your life and still have time for lots of committees and hobbies, go for it. But if you need to increase your income, maybe a class or second job should come first.

How? Resign today or the next time your membership comes up for renewal. Begin now to identify your successor and groom him or her. If this activity is not clearly linked to your most important personal and/or professional success values, consider phasing yourself out. You have more important things to do.

Ask yourself: Am I having so much fun, making so many valuable contacts, or learning so many valuable skills that this membership is worthwhile?

> *Tip*
> *Don't drift away from the group; tell people you are*
> *resigning and why. Very nicely of course. They'll*
> *respect you for it, and no nasty rumors will start.*

Curtail excess work. Are you working so much that your life is out of balance? Would you be better off getting perspective on your life, volunteering for something new, or investing in your family and friends? If you have a busy, demanding job and still feel connected with those you care about, good for you. But if you feel yourself becoming isolated or feel your health slipping, maybe personal time should be taken seriously for a while.

How? Track your time over the next month and see where it is going. How many days do you work overtime? Come home late for dinner? Work at night? Begin now to say no to future requests and set limits. Write down your important priorities, place the list on your desk, and phase out what doesn't apply. You have more important things to do.

Ask yourself: Am I concentrating so hard on my job that my personal life is suffering? Is that what I really want?

Tip
Give your boss some warning. Request a meeting and tell him or her that you plan some changes in the future and want to brainstorm how you can reinvent yourself and your workload.

Fresh Approaches

Here are some suggestions for new things to try. Experiment and see what works for you.

Change your evening routine. For many people, an untapped resource consists of the television hours from 8 to 10 p.m. This is one of your best opportunities to create an hour of joy and start a project you can hardly wait to begin. When dinner is over and you are settling into your evening routine, consciously remind yourself that you have a choice about how you will spend the next two hours.

How? Give up television reruns and poor-quality shows. Use the television listings to determine when you will turn the set on. For example, if you really enjoy a *Seinfeld* rerun, watch it. But then turn off the set the instant it is over so that you don't end up watching a bird show if you really don't care about birds. Start with one night a week. Over time you'll progress painlessly, taking back two or three nights a week for yourself.

Ask yourself: It's eight o'clock, and I have two hours to spend. What do I want to do now?

> *Tip*
> *Buy a minute timer and set it for five minutes. Then work on your project for that long. Give yourself permission to stop after five minutes if it's not fun. But I bet you won't! Often when you feel tired, you are really bored and starting something will revive you.*

Create concentration areas for personal and work items. This tip is useful for everyone but dedicated to those who work at home. For many people an ideal setup is a blending of personal and professional life, with both being delightful. A day is very integrated, and both personal and professional tasks are done as they make sense; there is no real separation. This is fine as long as it works. But sometimes one or the other requires higher priority or gets out of balance. The resulting undone piles of work have procrastination and guilt written all over them.

How? Separate your work life from your personal life. Ideally, you have separate rooms. But if you use the same desk for both work and personal management, set up two different inbaskets, two to-do lists, two different time blocks, and even two calendars. Accept the fact that certain things in your world are always going to be undone. Don't let your work drag down your personal life and take away the joy and satisfaction that come from completing other tasks.

Ask yourself: Am I procrastinating instead of working? Where can I relocate my distractions?

> **Tip**
> *Take a fresh look at underused areas of your office, cubicle, apartment, or house. Who says a bookcase is just for books? That a rarely used dining room wouldn't make a great home office?*

Create project kits. Make your tasks easy to do by getting everything you will need in one place. This way you have eliminated one of your favorite excuses, which is: "Guess I'll do this later because I can't find ____ or ____." This is a one-time investment in yourself that is definitely worth the effort.

How? Make a list of what you need and pull it all together. Buy additional tools, such as a stapler, highlighter, pencil, and ruler, if necessary. If you're over 40, add an extra pair of inexpensive reading glasses. Keep everything for the task in one place. Then start your project, finish it, and put your kit away. What a great way to have a feeling of satisfaction and completion. This is a no-guilt idea.

Ask yourself: What activity can be assembled into a "kit"?

> **Tip**
> *Use a briefcase, plastic bag, or container that has happy memories for you. You'll get a double delight every time you start your project.*

Reward yourself for a job well done, or at least done. As a procrastinator you spend a lot of time beating yourself up. How about a new approach in which you set up a system to reward yourself for being a real go-getter. The secret is to take it easy on yourself and reward any movement forward. You say you actually did look up a phone number? Great. Now allow yourself to schedule that lunch with the coworker you've been eager to meet. If you have ever trained a dog, you know how pitifully eager to please they are for a mere tidbit of liver. I mean a piece so small, you can hardly see it. As part of the animal kingdom, try a similar program on yourself.

How? Schedule something you enjoy. Promise yourself a walk around the park on your way home, or climb up three flights of stairs for mental refreshment. Buy a very healthy but tasty cookie and put it on your desk to tempt you as a treat for finishing. Allow yourself to neaten a file or read a professional journal. You are on top of things; you deserve it.

Ask yourself: What mental bribe can I use to entice myself?

Tip
Tell your boss or a friend about your progress.
How else are they going to know?

Accept that your choice is to do nothing and accept the consequences. Sometimes what you are procrastinating about isn't worth the effort to complete. The fact is that for the last several days, weeks, months, or years you haven't _____ (fill in your own blank here) and your world has kept on turning. Rather than beating yourself up, perhaps it's time to finally put your fantasy of finishing _____ to rest.

How? Take a hard look at the consequences of what you're not doing. Is your career success, health, or a personal relationship affected? If not, maybe it's time to let go of this "should" and give yourself permission to pursue that hour of joy that will give you so much pleasure.

Confessions of a procrastinator

Mary was in charge of preparing the quarterly financial statements for a small business. This task was so daunting that she dreaded the third month of every quarter just thinking about it. So she created a quarterly report kit for herself. She took a briefcase from a conference she had attended and enjoyed. Then she put in an extra copy of the last quarter's financial statements (marked "Reference" across the top) and prior tax return copies. As the quarter rolled along, she added mass mailings and new instruction sheets from the tax agencies. She wrote down and tossed into the briefcase any questions that popped into her mind. She realized she spent a lot of time adjusting inventory, so she kept her working notes on what to do about that too. She also added a ruler and highlighter to make her line-item reviews easier. When the time to begin the financials arrived, she was ready.

Mary reports that her project was a success. She found that not having to hunt down her most frequently needed items made her task more mentally pleasant and less time-consuming. Plus putting that briefcase away when everything was done was a moment of closure and joy.

Ask yourself: What will be the impact on my life if I just abandon this idea or project and move on to something else?

> *Tip*
> *Don't seek other people's approval to abandon a*
> *project. Strip away all false pretenses and wishful*
> *thinking and decide for yourself.*

Try a LIVELY approach. Finally, here is a way to change your frame of reference that I developed for myself some years ago. Remember, the basic premise of this book is that you always have a choice: to do something or to do nothing. If you choose to do something, you refine your options in regard to what something is. Here is a technique to help you do such a review. I call it the LIVELY approach.

How? Every time I felt myself procrastinating or stuck, I used my own name to remind me that I had at least six choices. My self-talk was: "Lynn, quit running around like a chicken with its head cut off. Instead, sit down, breathe deep, and take a LIVELY approach." Feel free to use my name, or next time you're stuck somewhere in traffic, see what you can come up with by using your own.

Picture your situation. Then mentally go through the following options and see what fits. Feel free to use more than one or to jump off in an entirely different direction. This is just a way to order your thinking. Can you

L: Leave things alone for now. Move on and accept the status quo. Realize that things probably will stay the way they are, and if that's acceptable, just get on with your life.

I: Imitate what someone else is doing. Think about the smartest person you know (or would like to know) and imagine how he or she would handle this situation. Then do that.

V: Very careful study.* Is the fact that you are procrastinating a survival mechanism? Maybe unconsciously you suspect that what you should do is wrong. The only way to find out is to back off and do some sort of study. *Tip:* If the dollar amount is over $500, consider a study.

E: Experiment. Give yourself permission to try something totally new. How about a "trial period," a six-week time to experiment during which you suspend all judgment? Promise yourself you'll make a decision after that.

L: Later.* Sometimes your life is in such crisis that you consciously decide you have to put things off till later. If that's the case, face the facts. Get out your calendar and move this project forward three months.

Y: You do it. Open your personal database and scan it till a name pops up. Say out loud, "I want you to do this." See how that feels and see if delegation, sharing, or a team approach is a possibility.

---

*I know a verb is missing, but my acronym would have broken down if I had added one. Remember, the object isn't perfection but action. If I can use an imperfect motivating device, so can you.

> *Remember*
> The best way to stop procrastinating is to turn it into a nonissue, something you don't do very much. To do that, some things you will want to do more of, some things you will want to do less of, and some things you will want to do differently. Your challenge is to mix and match the approaches, constantly increasing the number of techniques that work for you.

CHASE AWAY THOSE CLOUDS OF UNFINISHED BUSINESS

To overcome procrastination, you have to behave like a nonprocrastinator. Reach for a piece of paper right now. Tear off a strip and insert it between the pages of a tip you want to try. Jot a key word about the tip across the top of the strip so that you know why you marked the page. Take the rest of the paper and jot a few notes to yourself. Get out your calendar or the Yellow Pages and make a phone call.

What clouds of unfinished business are hanging around your mind, your day, your life? Begin today to chase those dreary old clouds away and expand your horizons. Unlike the weather outside, your internal meteorological condition is up to you. Use these tips to create sunshine, a gentle breeze, and calm seas for yourself. What could be a better use of your time? You deserve it.

And now, turn the page for a mental checkup.

3 WHY DO YOU PROCRASTINATE?

C ongratulations. You've taken the first step in breaking the cycle of procrastination. You have broken the cycle of inactivity and done something. Your project may not be finished, but it is well under way. You've started your research, made that first phone call, or gotten that dreaded meeting over with. Doesn't it feel good? Learn to congratulate yourself for a job well done. It's an example of those small motivators referred to in Chapter 2. Besides, who else is going to give you those well-deserved strokes?

PROCRASTINATION: IT'S ALL IN YOUR HEAD

Did you find that when you finally got started and did the deed, what you had to do wasn't really that hard? Most people do; the dread is far worse than the act itself. As my grandmother used to say, "It's so easy to work yourself into a *tizzy*." Which takes us to the next phase of your progress: figuring out why you let yourself get into a tizzy. This chapter will concentrate on you, your head, your heart, and what you are thinking and feeling, not on the external situation.

Imagine yourself trying to find your way down a mountain trail in the dark with a headlamp whose batteries are fading. You keep tripping over tree roots and sharp rocks. Your progress is very slow. Finally you stop and put in fresh batteries, and voilà, the path is obvious. That's what this chapter will do: provide a place for you to pause and insert fresh mental batteries so that your route is more clearly illuminated.

Tip

Chanting "I am not a procrastinator" is a short-term fix. Procrastination is complex, and denying what you are isn't going to help you break the cycle. Acknowledge the challenge you face. Instead tell yourself, "I am a capable human being who is going to _____ (whatever that discrete first step is for you) before I go home, go out to lunch, or call my friend." Then take three deep breaths, picture the hour of joy you will have earned, and move one small step forward.

PROCRASTINATION VERSUS PRIORITIES

Life is confusing. Putting things off is sometimes good, sometimes bad. Sometimes, you procrastinate because you don't want to start something; other times, because you don't want to stop something,

When you consciously choose to put something off—you are not procrastinating—you are setting priorities, making a deliberate choice about what is important, and acting accordingly. That is adult behavior that you feel good about. Procrastination occurs when you don't consciously choose to put something off but don't choose to do something else either. You are passive, in limbo, waiting for—well, actually you're not sure exactly what you are waiting for. This failure to choose to either act or not act is an anxiety-producing situation. It's no wonder you don't feel good about procrastination; it's a recipe for distress.

Further complicating the picture, people see the same situation differently. What is important to me may not be important to you, and vice versa. Have you ever impatiently waited for a report from a coworker who was late because he had to finish a rush job for his boss? What he defines as a priority you call poor planning, procrastination, or the failure to start early enough. The fact that you sense this confusion marks you as a very smart person, one who is aware of nuance and complexity.

Tip
Reduce confusion in yourself and others by clearly stating when you are procrastinating, when you have a different priority, and when you are uncertain about what to do. Your coworkers' stress level will go down when they clearly understand what you are doing. After all, they won't know until you tell them.

A NONPROCRASTINATOR INSIDE AND OUT

To live an interesting life, you have to like yourself. To like yourself, you have to be a nonprocrastinator inside and out. That means that what you do (your behavior) and what you believe, feel, and think are basically the same. Therefore, while taking action is an important aspect of being a nonprocrastinator, it's only half the equation. Now your challenge is to integrate your internal processes with your behavior. When you succeed, procrastination truly becomes a nonissue.

Respect this part of your self-improvement process. Thinking and feeling are invisible and intangible but nonetheless very real. Honing your mental skills, the same way you hone your computer skills will make you more successful, especially since so few people invest energy in improving this part of their personal packages.

The certainty, the knowledge, that you are doing the right thing is a quieting and very centered feeling. You know in a way that no one can shake, that you are doing what is right for you and those you care about. And this certainty gives you the courage to do what's difficult. It also means you can accept change more easily. Sure, you quiver a little, that's human. But when your department gets merged, your company is sold, your boss is transferred, a friend moves, or (add your item here), you know you will somehow manage and probably come out okay. You may end up facing in a different direction, perhaps, but one with interesting new horizons.

MIND-SETS: THE SECRET TO SUCCESS

I call the combination of mental and emotional processes mind-sets. They include how you think, your attitudes, what you believe, and your assessment of reality; they establish the foundation for how you feel about yourself. Think about it. What you feel in your heart influences the self-talk that runs through your head, and vice versa. Your mind is a powerful place.

Combining strong, realistic, and powerful mind-sets with a bias toward action will enable you to succeed beyond your wildest expectations. Remember Sang who quit smoking? The reason he succeeded was that his mind-set shifted to that of a nonsmoker. His logical mind knew it was the right thing to do, in his heart he wanted to do it, he knew how (don't light up), and when the strong emotional component of fear of getting ill like his father was added, his mind-set was such that he couldn't fail.

Improving your mind-sets will also give you an internal support system to count on when you are anxious and afraid. But the interesting thing is, the stronger you get, the less often you are anxious or afraid, because you know you can count on yourself. You respect your own capabilities—physical, emotional, and mental. You are the master of your own domain.

What's going on in *your* head? Let's examine mind-sets that can get you into trouble, followed by a new approach. Some mind-sets you will be conscious of, but others are more subtle, and you may have to look deep inside yourself to see if they might possibly relate to you. If you find yourself getting defensive, look hard! The categories are dangerous delusions, self-defeating self-talk, passing the buck, and hidden traps.

Dangerous Delusions

You probably don't want to hear this, but I'm going to ask you anyway: Are you kidding yourself? If so, procrastination can harm you. See if you are making these assumptions. If you are, maybe it's time for a reality check. That will get you going!

Are you procrastinating because you believe the following?

It'll probably work out okay. Sometimes things do work out okay, but not always. The reality is that sometimes your hopes, wishes, and dreams don't come true. The balance here is between faith, patience, and denial. More often things work out when you help fate along. Particularly if you are procrastinating about money, misunderstandings with people, or issues with other major life consequences, take a hard look at reality. Once you accept that you have a problem, you can face the worst-case scenario (which probably won't happen either). Now you're in a position to do some planning.

New approach: Be more realistic. Ask yourself what risks will increase if you wait. Let's say you're a small-business owner who notices an invoice payment that is overdue. Instead of assuming that everything will be okay, change your thinking by stating, "I give myself permission to let this overdue account ride for one more week with the assumption that the check will probably arrive. I will review the account next Thursday and, if the check isn't here by then, refuse to make any more shipments starting on May 15 if necessary."

> *Tip*
> *When you tell yourself, "Things will probably work out okay," add, "But if I am not certain of that by (a specific date), I will definitely do _____."*

Why try? I can't do anything about _____ (whatever it is). Give a deep, heartfelt groan and think: Poor, poor, pitiful me. Stop. That's enough pity party. Maybe you can do something. Don't let yourself become overwhelmed by the big picture; that will exhaust you before you start. Lower your sights. Identify one small thing you can do something about and concentrate on that. Doing so will help you regain a sense of control and remind you of the power you have.

New approach: Ask yourself what you can do right now. For example, perhaps you want to take a leave of absence for an extended vacation but you hear that the company's policy does not permit such a thing. Instead of giving up without trying, say, "I think I'll call HR for a copy of that policy and read it myself. I'll also have my boss read it and look for areas of flexibility."

> *Tip*
> *If you truly can't do anything about a situation, change your mind-set to one of acceptance. Change the "I can't _____" to "Company policy is _____." You can't win them all, and the situation was not set up to harass you personally. What other interesting thing can you concentrate on instead?*

This is the way I am. Do you have trouble starting a project because "that's just the way you are"? Self-acceptance is a delicate balance between what you are and what you could be. If you tip too far toward liking yourself as you are, you may become complacent and smug and fail to grow. If you tip too far toward never being satisfied, you're too hard on yourself and possibly bitter about what you're not. Your goal is to like yourself as you are while expanding your possibilities for growth. The world is changing, and so are you.

New approach: Change your self-talk. This is the way you were until *now.* Do you want to be different? If so, your challenge is what to do next. You can change; people do it all the time. You picked up this book, didn't you? You're already on your way. For example, perhaps you want to learn Spanish but think of yourself as "not good with languages." Change your thinking to: "I'm moderately bilingual. After all, I know the word for *beer* in Spanish. I think I'll double my vocabulary and learn how to order wine too. Wow, a 100 percent improvement! Next month I'll learn how to order vegetables."

Tip

In addition to observing that "This is the way I am," add, "And I like or want to improve this part of me." Observing how you feel about yourself will help you break out of that feeling of complacency and start moving.

Nobody cares; there's no reward for finishing this task. Question yourself carefully. Is this true? If so, see the previous discussion on busywork and officially abandon your task. But check with your boss first and broaden your definition of a reward. Perhaps your reward is that your life or the company runs more smoothly. *Idea:* Make a note to discuss the task at your next performance review. Can it be done less often? Not at all?

New approach: Cease to judge. Simply say, "It's time to finish this report. Once I'm done I can start (a more fun job)." Also ask yourself how you can make your task more bearable. Specifically identify the thing you dislike the most and challenge yourself to view it differently or to take steps to improve things.

> *Tip*
> *As a small-business owner and supervisor for many years, I have observed that many people underestimate the importance of what they do. Especially in these days of running lean, very few unnecessary tasks are permitted anymore. Just for fun, think about your effort and how many people it affects. You might be amazed how many others are counting on you.*

I haven't started because I'm so busy.   If you really are busy and juggling priorities, fine. But if you believe you are busy when you really lack self-discipline, watch out. You are only fooling yourself, and it's time to quit. This is a very dangerous self-delusion, because while other people may be polite to your face, your reputation is spreading. In the short term you can get out of a task, but in the long term, because no one wants to work with you, you'll miss the interesting opportunities that come along. There's no need to make a big deal of this; just quietly change your strategy and you'll soon be a welcome part of the team.

New approach: The next time you tell yourself you can't start a project because you are "so busy," stop in your tracks and ask yourself what has you so busy. Ask yourself which project has a bigger payoff. If necessary, quickly finish or set aside what you've already started and move along.

> **Tip**
> *If you have fewer responsibilities than others do and still feel busy, go on personal alert. You may be expanding small tasks to fill large blocks of time that loom before you. There's no need to do that. You are lucky to have choices about how you will spend your time. Instead, take a class, give of yourself, go to the library, talk to an interesting person, or challenge yourself to find something new and fun to do.*

> **Tip**
> *Have you become obsessed? Every once in a while everybody lets some part of his or her life get out of proportion. If you have spent more than a month on a task, ask yourself, Is this out of control? Is it keeping me from starting other important things I need to do? If so, define what "good enough" is, and when you reach that point, quit.*

I just don't have the time.   Lack of time is a subset of being too busy. Of course you already know that your day is as long as everybody else's. Time is discussed in greater detail in Chapter 5.

Why start? This work will just have to be redone anyway. The world is a messy place, and much of what you do will have to be redone. So what? High-powered consultants get paid a lot of money to come in and help people with "continuous improvement." If it's okay for them, it's okay for you. Your job is to move the project as far along as you can and then let the next person contribute. You aren't doing anything wrong. You are part of the development cycle.

CHAPTER THREE

The book *Jurassic Park* by Michael Crichton has a wonderful description of chaos theory, which is often applied to weather. Have you ever noticed that a long-range forecast covers just a few days? Chaos theory postulates that the wings of a butterfly flapping in Japan cause wind currents that affect the weather in San Francisco. The point is that the messiness and unpredictability of the world are bigger than you. Take responsibility for what you can fix and shrug your shoulders at the rest. Ease up on yourself and enjoy this crazy place for what it is.

New approach: Don't judge your task. Just nibble away at it. For example, you might say, "I don't know where to start, so I will do a brain dump and write down what I know in no particular order. Then I will review my thoughts and revise them into some sort of sequence, perhaps sorted by date, perhaps grouped by department. Then I'll pass my draft along to my coworkers to review. It'll be interesting to see their viewpoint."

Question: Who can help you?

Self-defeating Self-talk

Are you procrastinating because you are sabotaging yourself from the very beginning? See if the phrases below sound familiar and see what you can do to replace them.

Are you procrastinating because you are saying the following?

I don't want to do this task.   If you just plain don't want to do something, your thinking is vague. "I don't want to" is a summary statement. Force yourself to go deeper. What precisely is it you don't want to do? For example, are you avoiding changing the copier toner because it might get your new white shirt dirty? Now, that's a specific you can work with. Once you identify precisely what you don't want to do, you can either accept that you have to do it anyway and get it over with or make new plans. In this case, maybe you can borrow a coat from somebody in maintenance or plan to wear an older outfit tomorrow.

Confessions of a procrastinator

One of my early jobs was working for the assistant city manager from hell. My first assignment was to do a study of the city's fringe benefit package: How much did health insurance cost, were the vacation benefits in line with what other cities provided, what could be improved, and so on? I didn't know anything about fringe benefits, but I worked like a beaver for a month, scurrying to different departments and collecting information.

I assembled my report and triumphantly delivered it to my boss. He flipped through it and asked who else had seen it. "Why, no one," I replied naively, "I didn't want to bother anybody." With a sneer he threw it back and told me at a minimum to run it by the city clerk, the budget director, and the human resources manager. I was simply astonished. It never entered my mind that it was acceptable, let alone desirable, to involve others like that. Teamwork wasn't taught in my college; working together was called cheating.

I dutifully made my appointments, presented my report, and was astonished at the insights and wisdom my coworkers provided. They were nice about it too, gently correcting my misperceptions. I added concurrence lines for their signatures both to give them credit and to show my boss I really had talked to them.

As you can tell, I still think my boss was a jerk. But I give him credit for teaching me the power of "review and comment." There's no reason to procrastinate because your work will have to be redone. Just get started on a draft and let other smart people help you finish.

New approach: Focus on the outcome you are eager to achieve. You might say something like, "These copies sure are faint. They'll look a lot better with fresh toner in the photocopier and the rollers cleaned. Tomorrow I'll wear that old sweatshirt and get the thing all fixed up."

> **Tip**
> *If a task is no fun or no option is appealing, ask yourself if waiting will make things disappear or get any easier. If it will not, tell yourself you might as well get it over with.*

I don't have a firm due date. Here is a variation of the good student, get-into-a-crunch mind-set we discussed earlier. This is one of the easier fixes. The challenge here is to set a deadline for yourself or work with a boss to set one for you. Note that I didn't say "your" boss. Even a friend can be the "boss" who holds you accountable. The main thing is to get out your calendar and start setting due dates. Doing so will put this project on schedule and get it started.

New approach: Start a big folder where you put all your miscellaneous projects. Once a week go through the folder and consciously ask yourself: "When is this project due? Do I need to start it this week?" Pull out the "this week" projects and schedule them. And with a clear conscience put the folder (and any guilt) away until next week's review.

> **Tip**
> *To help you concentrate on finishing your most important task, start a folder and label it "Things to Do Once _____ Is Finished." Then toss ideas to research, calls to make, things to repair, and so forth, in that folder. That way you know you won't forget to do those odd jobs but will still focus on your big job.*

I have too many distractions.   Do you find yourself scattered and unable to concentrate? If so, you are probably surrounded by too many distractions. The result is that you are rarely able to finish anything. Some jobs are like this; if yours is one of them, can you change your hours so that you come in earlier and nobody will know you are there? Your challenge is to set your own limits and learn to tune out a lot of what is going on around you.

New approach: Say to yourself: "I will not permit my brain to receive any input until I have worked one hour on the _____ job." When someone comes up to you, look vague and uninterested. Also, can you figure out a way to leave your current work space and find a quiet corner? Cafeterias, lobbies, libraries, toilet stalls, and cars are all good spots. Bundle up your work, disappear for half an hour, and see what you get done. You will amaze yourself with your progress.

Tip

If you are easily distracted, the next time you start to jump up before you have finished your current job, lightly tap yourself on the wrist and say "Down." Then, when you finish your task, say to yourself, "Okay, you can get up now." I learned this trick while training my dog Scanner, and I now use it to train myself. The command "Sit" also works. Be sure to have your treats handy so you can reward yourself for good behavior. I have a new hardback book I paid full price for that I will allow myself to start reading when this chapter is finished.

I am not organized.   If this is you, stop beating yourself up right now and instead go to a bookstore. There are many wonderful paperbacks on how to be better organized. Your challenge is to find one that fits your style. You are not the first person to face this issue, so don't reinvent the wheel. Learn from other people's research (and mistakes).

New approach: Say to yourself: "Where shall I begin?" Take everything you have so far and dump it on a table. Then pick up any item and place it at the top left of the table. Pick up a second thing and see if it relates to the first thing. If so, put it on top of the first item, or start a second pile. Continue sorting and assembling like items. Then decide which of those piles reflects what has to be done first. Start there.

> ### *Tip*
> *Writing something, for example, a letter, report, or application, involves four parts: assembling the required information (if any), making notes about what to say and how to say it, writing a draft, and editing the final copy. Which stage are you in? Today, do one of the parts.*

> ### *Tip*
> *If you have to fill out forms, photocopy them before filling out anything. Use the blank photocopy as a draft form; after editing, copy your work onto the original. Be sure to make another copy of the final document for your records. This technique removes the fear of messing up an original.*

Passing the Buck

Are you procrastinating because of other people? Before we go any further, I want to say that you are absolutely right: Other people are exasperating. If it weren't for *them*—bosses, teammates, coworkers, clients, customers, significant others—the world would be an easier place to live in. You and I would do things right, and things would run smoothly. But alas, sometimes I confess I'm on somebody else's list of exasperating people, and I bet every once in a while you are too. Let's look at some of the reasons why others may be causing you to procrastinate and what you can do about it.

Are you procrastinating because you think the following things?

I shouldn't have to do this; it's not fair.   The reality is that life isn't fair. Life, work, and the universe just are. What that means is that some days, weeks, months, and years flow more smoothly than others do. Every once in a while things pile up, and you may be the one tapped to do more than your share. First of all, own up to your resentment; it's honest. Write down how you feel and tuck it away in a safe place. Say every terrible thing you can think of; this is called venting and is emotionally healthy. Once your anger has been acknowledged, take a deep breath and get started. You want to get this over with and go on to more fun things.

New approach: Objectively describe the situation to yourself. Then say, "Obviously, _____ feels I am a capable person or he wouldn't have asked me to do this. I might as well get started. Besides, I'm building up credits for when I'm sick or want time off."

Tip

If this overload involves a coworker, jot down a few facts while the incident is still fresh in your mind. The next time you meet with your boss, look at your notes and see if the issue still strikes you as one to be discussed. By waiting for a regularly scheduled meeting to raise the issue, you'll be calmer, have a better perspective on how the overload caused you delays, and be able to come up with good recommendations for how to rearrange things the next time.

They haven't told me what to do. Are you procrastinating because you don't know precisely what to do or how to do it? Here is a great opportunity for you to grow. First, think about who you can ask for further directions. Second, have faith in yourself and your own abilities. Third, take a chance and figure things out for yourself. What an opportunity to tell yourself what to do.

New approach: Don't wait for someone else to tell you what to do; instead, take charge of yourself. Say to yourself: "This is scary, but here is a chance for me to grow. I will just go ahead and start this project. The worst thing I can be is wrong, and the consequences don't appear to be too serious."

Caution: Use common sense. Sometimes the consequences are serious. In that case, do routine work or take your coffee break early and come back when someone is around to help you.

Tip

One thing successful people learn very quickly is that rewards come to those who use their best judgment and try something, not to those who stand around waiting. You might make a mistake, but it is offset by the effort, initiative, and goodwill you showed. Ask yourself if making a mistake could cost more than $25 or one hour of time. If not, go ahead, you smart person. Do what you think makes sense. Then fill your boss in when he or she returns.

It's someone else's mistake. Until you are perfect, people are going to be covering for you, redoing your mistakes, and having to work around your less-than-perfect performance. The fact is, you probably don't even know how often this is happening because people are too nice to tell you. Now it's your turn to return the favor. Just quietly pick up the pieces and help out. Go ahead and get started; this is your chance to be a hero. And adjust your halo, you angel; it's glowing.

New approach: Make yourself valuable as part of the solution. Say to yourself: "We have a crisis around here. What an opportunity this is for me to try something new, get credit with the boss, or _____(your reason here). I might as well get started."

Hidden Traps

Here are some observations I have made of procrastinators who don't realize they are procrastinating. It's hard to change a mind-set when you don't know you have it. Start by noticing these qualities in others. Don't judge; just look for signs. Then look at yourself. Once you catch yourself doing the same thing, you can change.

Are you procrastinating because you think the following things?

When this is finished, you don't have anything better to do. Have you ever met someone who can stretch out a chore forever? You know, the ones who take three months to pull income tax records, need two weeks to pack for a one-week trip, and contin-

Confessions of a procrastinator

Althea was working on her income tax records. She was a meticulous type who liked to create all sorts of subtotals. For example, she subtotaled medical bills and charity expenses. Then she realized she took the standard deduction, so why bother? She told herself that what she had was good enough and that she'd be better off getting out in the sunshine.

ue to look for the best price even after an item has been purchased. The failure to finish in a timely fashion is a form of procrastination and a trap you want to climb out of because you are missing an hour of joy that could be used for a coffee break or walk.

New approach: Notice if other people seem to finish the same task in less time than you need. If that is the case, say to yourself: "I am making this task harder than it needs to be. I will work one hour on this project today. I will no longer _____(specify something you won't do). Then I will shift to _____(something new)."

The task is too hard. This is the reverse of the above. Sometimes a task is beyond you and you are procrastinating

Confessions of a procrastinator

Alan worried about doing his taxes, but he had a friend who worked for IRS who assured him, "The tax forms are easy. Every American can prepare his own return." Alan believed him and scheduled April 13 to do his own taxes. As he looked at the forms for limited partnerships, home office deductions, and capital gains, his heart sank. He was in over his head. The job was too hard for him. He realized it would take him a long time to figure this out. He also realized that even though he struggled this year, he wouldn't use the information again until next year, by which time he would have forgotten everything. Mumbling at his friend, he went down to H & R Block with a cry for help. The next year he didn't even consider doing his own taxes. Instead he concentrated on making sure his retirement account was correct.

for good reason. It doesn't make sense for you to proceed; and you sense that. If this is the case, stop right now. You probably know best; trust yourself. Abandon your project, get help, or get training.

New approach: Reorder your priorities. Say to yourself: "This is a project I really want to master. But not now. Until I _____ (finish whatever), I am taking it off my to-do list. Now is not the right time for me. I have better things to do."

You have acquired some bad habits.   Go back to your childhood. Are you a little too much like your mother or father? Is it time to change? For example, perhaps your family always put up a Christmas tree on December 24. You may have picked up an unexamined assumption that festive events lose their fun if you start planning too soon. Now, when it's your job to plan the Christmas party, you have to run around at the last minute getting things organized and are too tired to enjoy yourself. You realize you want to start your planning sooner. It's time to let go of bad habits that don't add to your pleasure.

New approach: Consciously say to yourself: "I have a choice about how to live my life. I choose to discard this dysfunctional behavior. Instead I will start earlier next time." Then get out your calendar and pencil in your start dates. Maybe you can't do much about what is already done, but you can vow not to procrastinate the next time. That's okay. Forgive yourself and think how much better the next go-round will be.

Remember
Turning procrastination into a nonissue takes more than just changing your behavior. You also need to work on your mind-set—what you think and feel about putting things off. Examine yourself for dangerous delusions, self-defeating self-talk, passing the buck, and hidden traps. Once you see what you are doing to yourself, you can change.

> ### *Confessions of a procrastinator*
>
> Luther always did his taxes on April 14, and it was stress time, yelling at the kids and fussing at his wife. He finally remembered that his parents did their taxes on April 14, and it was stress time for them too. He remembered being told to stay out of the way and be quiet. Once he saw a pattern, he told himself he hadn't liked it when he was a kid and wasn't going to repeat the same negative behavior as an adult. The next year, he started preparing his taxes on February 15 when his W-2's came in; he was done by February 28. He liked himself, and his family liked him too.

FACE YOUR FEARS

This chapter presented many different mind-sets that can contribute to procrastination. Certainly not all pertain to you, but one or two of them should cause you to reflect. Take a minute right now and make some notes to yourself. Don't you feel encouraged that you're not alone in this struggle? Other people have made progress, and you can too. Start today.

Also note on your calendar that you should review this chapter in six months. You'll find that some items now appear irrelevant (because you've already mastered them), but another item or two will probably be worth your attention. You are a growing individual with new challenges to face.

Did you notice that this chapter did not include what is probably the most universal reason for procrastination? You guessed it: fear. Fear takes many forms and is the focus of Chapter 4. Turn the page and get ready to enter the Risk Zone!

4 SUCCESS MEANS ENTERING THE RISK ZONE

W hat if things don't work out?

If you are procrastinating because you are afraid of what might happen, this is the chapter for you. Your survival skills are on high alert because you smell risk: the risk of uncertainty, the risk of failure. The fear of risk is an honest one. Own up to it; it's a respectable part of you. The challenge is to understand it and keep it in perspective.

THINGS MIGHT GO WRONG

After all, you might do something and then find that

You were wrong

Your request was turned down

You looked foolish

You aren't good enough

You broke down and cried

The other person yelled at you

Reality isn't as good as your fantasy, and you miss your fantasy

You lost money

You got hurt

You hurt someone else

People don't like you anymore

You were right; you knew you couldn't do it

Add your reason here

Add the real, terrible, awful reason here

These outcomes are certainly possible, but take a look at that list. Have you noticed something about it? It's totally skewed in one direction, reflecting failure, pain, and loss. Every single option is a negative one.

Let's pause a minute and think things through. Does it make sense that the odds are 100 percent that what you do will turn out wrong *for sure*? I believe that kind of thinking is just as flawed as that of the person who believes nothing bad could ever happen to her or him. As a practical matter you rarely meet someone like that, because those people are isolated in a psychiatric facility for their own good, totally out of touch with reality.

You can predict few outcomes with absolute certainty. What you can do is

Face the worst-case scenario and see if you can live with that.

Estimate the odds that something will happen and see if you can live with that.

Improve your chances for success.

THEN AGAIN, THINGS MIGHT GO RIGHT

Let's take another look at that list. Have you also considered that you might do something and then find out that

You were right and your self-confidence grew

Your request was approved, although perhaps with modifications

You looked brave, strong, and human

You were good enough—just barely, but you made it

Your lip quivered, but you said your piece anyway

The other person yelled, but you stood your ground quietly and firmly

Reality exceeded your fantasy, and next time you will think bigger still

You made money or got a promotion

You didn't get hurt or you got hurt but survived

You didn't hurt someone else, or you did but it wasn't serious

People respect you or you decide to get new friends

You proved to yourself you can do it

Add your own dreams, possibilities and successes here

Some day you might even _____

Remember, if you don't overcome your procrastination, you know what will happen: nothing. Is that what you want?

THE GREATEST RISK OF ALL

I believe the greatest risk you face is to cling to the present or, worse yet, the past. Enjoy the present, for it is where you live. But keep getting ready for the future. This is how you grow. The world is changing, and if you deny that, you'll be left behind. Don't let that happen to you. You don't want to become one of those people you avoid—you know, the ones who bore you with conversations about "how it used to be" and "things will never be the same." You can't know the future, but you can continually prepare for it. What nobody might have told you is that it's fun! Taking chances and trying new things make life very interesting.

Change is subtle. It opens up opportunities for you all the time; you just have to grab them. First, of course, you have to recognize the opportunities change brings. Within the last year have you used new technology (for example, something with a computer or telephone), met a new person, or tried a new product? Of course you have, and those things are shaping you and your world. Think how those encounters will make your world different next year. Those are avenues of opportunity to pursue.

> *Tip*
> *Master one new computer program per year. Doing so will keep your mind flexible and your skills marketable. It's a fun way to grow.*

Change is also inevitable. Things will never be exactly the same again. Remember our earlier reference to chaos theory and butterfly wings? Butterfly wings are flapping somewhere in the world and will bring change to you too. Can you hear them?

LOST PRIDE IS A SMALL PRICE TO PAY FOR AN INTERESTING LIFE

Let's say you try something and you lose. Whatever you try doesn't work out. In the short term you probably will experience pain, loss, and humiliation. But those feelings are temporary and will fade. Not only that, they'll leave you stronger, more experienced, and wiser. The image I like is that of a willow tree: It bends and flexes in the winds but doesn't break. In the long run you'll learn what doesn't work, get ideas for what might work the next time, and have a very interesting experience that will make a great story once you can laugh about it—in a year or two.

The thing to remember about humiliation is that it is a hundred times more awful for you than for anyone else. The reality is that other people don't care about your embarrassment very much; they have their own lives to live. Sure, you may be the talk of the lunchroom for a day or two, but someone else is out there right now doing something perfectly ghastly that will the subject of discussion next week.

If you live your life governed by the need never to be humiliated, wrong, or embarrassed, you will miss much of what life has to offer. The only way to experience the satisfaction of joy, contentment, and exhilaration is to be willing to experience the other painful extremes. You can do it; you just have to put things in perspective. Read your daily newspaper; note that athletes and politicians lose every day, and very publicly. They hold their heads high and keep going; so can you.

Tip

If you think you might be the subject of lunchroom gossip because you took a chance and things didn't turn out as you hoped, prepare for it. Own up to what happened and direct the conversation the way you want it to go. Describe your own reactions; don't let the company gossip do it for you.

For example, if you lost a job everyone knows you wanted badly, tomorrow you march right into that lunchroom wearing your best outfit and say, "Well, I just found out Pam got the bookkeeping job I applied for [the truth]. I am disappointed [notice you are admitting a very specific, honest emotion], but she's very experienced in taxes and will be good [you're a pro and don't bad-mouth others]. I just heard about this class on managerial accounting, so I think I'll sign up for that. It sounds like fun [you're moving on]." The point is that the pain and humiliation will fade very quickly if you let them.

CHAPTER FOUR

IMAGINE SUCCESS

If you've been timid recently, it's easy to think too small. The following exercise is fun and will take you to a higher level. Think big. You deserve it.

Imagine Success

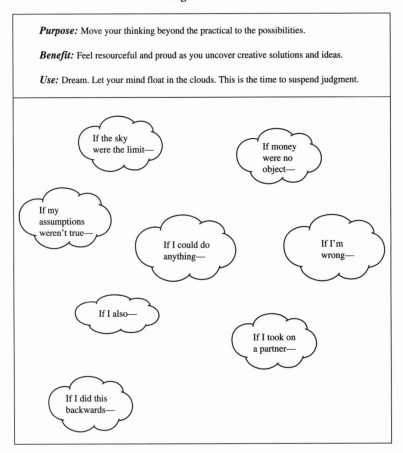

FACE THE WORST-CASE SCENARIO

If you are procrastinating because you are afraid of what might happen, there are two things to do. Step 1 is to imagine the absolutely most terrible, awful worst case ever. Step 2 is to figure out the more likely worst case and what you will do about it.

Step 1

To confront the absolutely most awful scenario possible, use a piece of paper and write it down. Once you do that, wonderful things happen in your brain. Your worst-case nightmare is now out in the open. You can see it, imagine it, and visualize it. Your worst case looks far different written down in daylight with phones ringing in the next cubicle or the cat on your lap than it does at 3 a.m. when you are quivering alone in your bed in the dark.

Go ahead. Get a piece of paper right now and label it across the top:

> If I do _____, the absolute worst thing that could happen to me is _____.

If you feel noble, add a second section:

> The absolute worst thing that could happen to others (the company, department, etc.) is _____.

Usually the worst thing you can come up with is "I'll die." If that's not likely to happen, back off to "I'll be permanently maimed or disabled." If your action doesn't include physical risk, other possibilities to consider are

> I'll never work again.
>
> I'll starve and have to eat cat food when I'm eighty.
>
> I'll be fired.

Work your way down the list until you start smiling. Isn't the drama of it wonderful? Don't you feel like you're in eighth grade again, exaggerating with your friends? Once you're laughing, you're well on the way to making a more realistic assessment of the worst case. You've faced your fears and discarded the ones that don't hold up well in the light of day. Do you feel your internal courage barrel filling up again?

Step 2

Crumble up that sheet of paper and start over. Write down a new worst-case scenario, one that more accurately reflects what might happen if things don't work out. Be as realistic as you can. Your emotions are now under control, and you can think more clearly. Good for you. Now you are imagining a future that has some chance of taking place.

In addition to the worst-case scenario, create one or two likely scenarios. Your thinking is at a peak now, and you really are doing a great job of using your mind to anticipate what might happen. Folks, this is fun. You are creating your own future. What could be a better use of your time?

Key question: Ask yourself, Can I live with this risk of the worst case? If the answer is yes, get going. You've got things to do. The rest of your life is waiting.

If the answer is no, cross the action off your to-do list for now, for a while, or forever. Be clear that you are also crossing off any possibility that you might succeed. You are closing a door. You are taking your life in a different direction, and it's one that is right for you.

If you can live with your worst case, do some more thinking. Brainstorm what you will do if the unwelcome event occurs and what you can do to prevent it from happening. Further refine your "this will probably happen" scenarios. This is called strategic planning and is well worth your time. Take good notes and date them. You'll have fun later seeing how things turn out.

Question: Have you worked through your worst-case fears?

ESTIMATE THE ODDS

After you convert your worst-case scenario to a more probable outcome, the next thing to do is figure out the odds: the probabili-

Confessions of a procrastinator

James and Reed had started a small business building electronic sensors, and the bank required them to pledge their house as collateral for a line of credit. They decided that they did not want to lose their house. That meant their company would grow more slowly than would those of their competitors who took bigger risks. They knew they would pay a price for being conservative, but it was what felt comfortable for them.

The first years were a real struggle, and Reed spent most Saturdays figuring out how much money the sales would bring in and when and how much the next month's payroll and bills would be. Every time the two considered growing their business, they sat down and first decided if doing so would put their house at risk. Then they made their decision accordingly. Sometimes a new product line or advertising campaign just had to wait. They also rented out a spare bedroom to get some additional cash.

Reed told me privately that when they had to pledge their house to the bank, she sat down all by herself and carefully considered the possibility that they might lose the house. She figured the worst case was that she would have to live in a tent. She loved hiking and backpacking and figured she could handle that worst case if it ever came down to that. She knew there were public showers at a nearby public marina. At one level she knew she was being ridiculous, but facing those worst-case fears gave her the courage to go on. Reed told me this story many years later, after she had a lot of money in the bank, and I can assure you she lived a very interesting life.

ty that your anticipated results will happen the way you expect. Part II of this book covers this type of thinking extensively and so only a basic approach will be presented here. But you know what? Most times the basic approach is good enough.

How do you estimate the odds that something will happen to you? What you "should" do is research, a careful study. You should go to the library, interview people, compile giant files, and do spreadsheets. Maybe you will create some impressive statistics— standard deviations or chi-squares. Does that sound exhausting? Yes. Are you going to do that? Probably not. Is there a simpler way? Yes, and let's talk about that.

Note that sometimes the risk is so high that a formal study is worth your effort. Buying a building, changing jobs, and spending a lot of money are examples of study candidates. But many times you procrastinate when a simple review will do.

Incidentally, if you ever get offered a job as an analyst (management, financial, budget, program, operations, etc.), take it. You will learn to do such studies and develop the rigor of thinking they entail. The experience will benefit you personally and professionally for the rest of your life.

If you are procrastinating because you aren't sure what your chances for success are, go away by yourself for one hour with a pencil and a pad of paper. You are going to create mental models, worksheets to help you think.

Your first mental model is figuring the odds. Across the top of the first sheet write down what you have to do and the probable outcome. Draw a line under that sentence or paragraph. Then create two columns. Label the left one "Why I Think This Will Happen." Label the right column "Why I Think This Won't Happen." This is a very messy process, but no one will see what you write so put down anything that comes to mind. There are no right or wrong answers, only your thoughts. Feel free to create additional sheets for different outcomes.

Other things you can mentally model include

What this will cost	What this will save
What could go right	What could go wrong
Who might help	Who might hurt
What will be fun	What will be hard
Your own pluses	Your own minuses

After you have finished the list, read it again. In each column circle the three most probable reasons (or four or two; you decide). Now take a hard look at the list. Some of those items are more important than others. Some of those things will happen for sure; others you're not certain of. If you want to, assign a number from 1 to 10 for each item, with 10 being the most certain. Total the numbers and see what that tells you. Your goal isn't to know everything, because that's impossible. Only hindsight is 20–20. Your goal is to get a sense of direction and become more clear about what, if anything, you should do.

Now do what makes the most sense. Remember, you always have the choice between doing something and doing nothing. If you choose to do something, what will it be? Also remember that it may make the most sense to get more information, or to wait a bit. That's okay if you use the time to learn something and improve your thinking.

IMPROVE YOUR CHANCES OF SUCCESS

Let's look at what you've already done. You've sat down and faced your worst-case fears and realized that you probably exaggerated the risk. You've created mental models and come up with likely scenarios. You've figured out the odds on whether something is going to happen.

Confessions of a procrastinator

Marsh worked for a garden supply company and
wanted to propose a new product idea—an automatic plant-watering device—to his boss. But he
didn't want to look like an idiot and be shot down.
In the past nobody took his ideas very seriously,
and now he was afraid to speak up. He sat on his
idea for several months. But company sales were
lagging, and he knew this product would help.

He tried a new approach. In the past he had simply
blurted out ideas in staff meetings. This time he
decided to do things differently. He did his homework and created his mental models. He wrote a
one-sentence description of the new device. He
looked through competitors' catalogs to see if similar products were available and examined suppliers'
catalogs to see what the parts might cost. He wrote
up a one-page description of what he had in mind.
He told his boss before the staff meeting that he
would like a few minutes to present an idea. To
make a long story short, Marsh was a hero. Not
only did people like his idea, his obvious concern
for the welfare of the group brought new energy
and commitment to the team. And he got to head
up the new project.

There's only one step remaining, and that's to spend a bit of
time figuring out what you can do to increase the odds in your
favor. Before doing that, I want you to pause and respect how powerful this process is. Do you realize that so far everything you have
done is in your head? You haven't made anybody mad, spent any
money, or embarrassed yourself. You haven't done anything
wrong, wasted time on anything that will have to be redone, or

made any false starts. Instead, you are doing things right. Once you take action, you will finish your task once and for all, knowing you did the best job you can. Think of the hours of joy that await you. This is exciting. And you can do this. Not perfectly, of course, but well enough.

To improve your own chances for success, take another piece of paper. Label it "Mental Model: Things I Can Do to Increase My Chances of Success." Examine every item you noted on your previous mental models and ask yourself, "What can I do now that will make me more likely to succeed later?" For example, your list might include two or three of the following.

Mental Model: Things I Can Do to Increase My Chances of Success include:

Earn a certificate

Prepare an estimate

Call another source

Review old files

Take an expert to lunch

Write out my request

Outline my thinking

Study a workbook

Get a testimonial letter

Request a second opinion

Ask for advice from my old boss

(What can you come up with?)

Finally, ask yourself whether you want to succeed badly enough to exert the effort. It's okay not to. But if you want something badly, work for it. Let some of the small things now occupying your time go. You can succeed if you make the effort. And effort is nothing scary, just a series of small steps. You can do it.

Confessions of a procrastinator

Raj was bored with his current job as a production supervisor and finally got tired of hearing himself complain about it. One day he saw a job listed on the bulletin board, and he wanted it. He decided to do things right.

First he got a copy of the job description. Then he pulled out his résumé. With those two items, plus a pencil and a tablet of paper he stopped at his neighborhood McDonald's restaurant one evening on his way home from work. The first part of his mental model was easy. He knew he could do this job and didn't see any risk there. His problem was lots of competition. So he decided to review his résumé to increase the odds in his favor. His mental model looked like this:

**Mental Model: Increasing My Chances
for Success on My Résumé:**

Job Duty	My Experience	What I Could Do
Supervise staff of 20	Supervise 5 people	List special assignments
Prepare budget	Prepare budget summary	Include copy of budget
Prepare annual report	Prepare quarterly report	Design a sample page
		Read old reports

As you can see, Raj worked hard. He wanted this new opportunity and did his homework, and it showed. He got the job.

EMOTIONAL OVERLAYS

Many times you procrastinate because of your emotions. The following mental model is designed to help you get those fears out in the open and see what they are doing to you. Just like your worst-case scenario, once you face your fears in the light of day, they often seem less threatening.

Emotional Overlays

Purpose: Work through emotions that might unduly influence your ability to think clearly. Every decision has an emotional aspect. Fear or denial of reality are particularly dangerous to your thinking.

Benefit: Reduce overreaction, denial, procrastination, and fear. Increase courage, clarity, determination, and fairness.

Use: Go to a private place and examine your heart and soul. Tear up and throw away when done. This is for your eyes only.

How I feel about this situation:

How this feeling might influence my ability to make a decision:

What I might do to overcome the power of this emotion so I can think more clearly:

SPECIAL CASE: YOU CAN'T SAY NO

Do you find it hard to say no to a request? Many people do. The reasons are complex, but if you keep digging, often it comes down to the fear that somebody won't like you. Saying no is a risk but one that you sometimes need to take. After all, if you're tactful, people will probably still like you. And even if they're a bit disappointed, what you're doing is increasing their respect for you and your respect for yourself.

You will be a procrastinator until you learn to say no appropriately. As long as you agree to all requests, you are letting other people govern your priorities. While your excuses may sound impressive, the reality is that you are not in control of your own destiny. Saying no doesn't mean you're a negative person; it means you know what you have to do now and you do it. Sure, you'll miss a few opportunities, but by concentrating on what's important, you're opening future doors for yourself.

> *Tip*
> *If you struggle with no, practice a phrase that is comfortable for you on the way home from work tonight. Then seek an opportunity to use it. For example, tell someone you need to resign from her committee or bow out of a meeting. Then, the next time someone catches you by surprise, you'll have a prepared response ready.*

Also, don't forget that wonderful phrase "Let me think about it." Saying that will buy you time to decide what makes the most sense.

Confessions of a procrastinator

Bill's life was exhilarating and crazy. He was a busy, important business executive who had something going on every minute. That was the good news. The bad news was that he rarely met his deadlines and was up till 3 a.m. on way too many nights. Just when he thought things were under control, he was asked to chair yet another committee. He never said no because it was his duty and he liked serving.

Finally he took a long hard look at how his grains of sand were passing through his hourglass. He realized that in addition to the sense of duty and fun, he didn't want to let anyone down. He hadn't yet confronted his need to be liked. He quit procrastinating, faced this key issue, and realized that this deeply rooted fear was out of proportion. He vowed to create the time to smell a few more roses and spend some of the money he had earned. The next time someone invited him for a special project, he said no. It was really hard, especially since the meetings were in Paris. But he finally was being true to himself.

TRIGGER POINTS

Some situations have more risk than others. Yet if you look around, you'll see people agonizing over trivia while they procrastinate on important issues.

Here is a five-point checklist to help you spot situations where your risk is high. Be careful when

1. *More than 10 percent of something is involved.* Whether it's time, money, product line, customer base, warranty problems, staff effort, or inventory—more than a 10 percent impact on any of these factors involves risk.

2. *The results will be hard to change.* Executing a formal lease, taking on a new partner, lowering morale with a layoff, and starting a new production line are all examples of situations that will be hard to change. Create your mental models before beginning.

3. *The impact of your actions will be long term.* Hiring a new manager, pulling money out of your savings account to start a new business, and switching computer systems are all examples of situations that have long-term implications.

4. *You are inexperienced in this area.* For example, your risk of failure is higher if you have never hired, fired, disciplined, evaluated a new opportunity, or worked at home. You've got to start somewhere. Just keep your eyes open.

5. *You care a lot about what happens.* If, even after telling yourself that you are being petty and ridiculous, the situation continues to gnaw at you, you are at risk. These are the situations where it is too easy to do nothing for a long time and then blow up, saying things you regret later. Own up to your feelings. Then move accordingly.

PUSH YOURSELF: COURAGE COMES FROM WITHIN

Most things you have to do each day are fun or easy; some are boring, and you do them because that's what maintaining your life requires. But some things are very, very difficult. The nonprocrastinator does them too. And that's you. You do the things that aren't fun because you know that until you do, you are stuck. You

Confessions of a procrastinator

Lumpo was 13 years old, and Ellen loved that calico cat dearly. Lumpo got her name because she was always there, a contented lump on whatever bed, chair, or couch Ellen was sitting. One day Ellen decided to add a puppy to her household. So she did, and that puppy was a handful of boundless energy and wiggly joy. The puppy loved Lumpo and wanted to play, to have them chase each other and be pals. The pup was never mean to the cat, just exuberant. Lumpo couldn't adjust. Her world was shattered.

The first accident Ellen ignored. Lumpo was just traumatized. I'm sure she got confused about where her litter box was, Ellen thought. But the accidents continued and got more frequent. Lumpo was starting to urinate on piles of dirty laundry beside the washing machine and finally on Ellen's bed. She was in misery. Ellen hoped things would get better but finally realized she had to act. She asked everyone she knew (and a few perfect strangers on the bus) to take the cat, but no one was willing as soon as she explained her problem.

For a month she procrastinated, and she knew it. She finally realized she couldn't have her house smell like cat urine; her beloved pet would have to be euthanized. Sobbing uncontrollably, she took her cat to the pound for that option because, as she explained, what if some unsuspecting family adopted her and then mistreated her when Lumpo urinated on their bed? Ellen told me she cried often and grieved for her cat for weeks. But she also explained that she never regretted what she did. "There was no win-win here. I don't even know if I was right. I simply did what I believed I had to do at the time. And I uncovered a strength in myself that I plan to use when I have to make other difficult decisions."

are stuck in a monotonous rut that you don't know how to get out of. You sense your life slipping by like sand through an hourglass, sand without any sparkle. You want to put the sparkle back in your life. And that's going to take courage.

Be courageous. Face what is worrying you, because until you do, you will stifle your life energy. I don't know how many days you have on this earth, but I don't want you to waste one of them. You are too special to spend any of your precious moments with dread, fear, and self-loathing. Figure out a way under, over, or around your challenges. Once you do, you will like yourself and free yourself up for many new adventures, interesting experiences, and successes.

When a decision is permanent, procrastination can provide that buffer zone to make sure you are doing the right thing. But when you know what to do, you might as well get it over with.

YOU GET A SECOND CHANCE; TAKE IT

I wish I could guarantee you that if you take a risk, everything will turn out okay. Nobody can do that, but what I can guarantee you is that you have far more second chances than you have imagined. If things don't go the way you hope, start over. Lick your wounds, reflect on your "learning experience," and find a new approach. You can do it; it's what puts sparkle in your life.

Remember

Things might go wrong. But don't forget that things also might go right. If you don't take chances, you know how things will turn out. But is that the way you want to live?

Confront your fears head on. If you do it in the daylight, you'll be able to sleep at night. Base your decisions on possible outcomes—both good and bad. Use mental models to increase your chances for success. As you enter the Risk Zone, savor your successes and learn to appreciate your failures; they teach you a lot and make you stronger. Life is a roller coaster; open your eyes and enjoy the ride.

5 OVERCOMING INERTIA: A BEGIN-ER'S CHECKLIST

Are you stuck?

Answer yes if you know what to do but still haven't done it. You continue to procrastinate, but you have made progress. You have faced your excuses and set them aside, recognized your fears and worked through them. Something is still stopping you.

Don't give up on yourself. Being stuck can be a very subtle situation. What this chapter will do is give you a checklist to help identify your missing links. Once you identify what you are missing, you can figure out how to get it. Consider this list carefully. Use it as a springboard to help you refine your thinking. Overcoming inertia, like everything else in life, is done one step at a time.

Many of these lessons have come from my 20 years of mountaineering. I've learned that the most formidable-looking summit can be reached one step at a time. But each mountain has its own strategy. Sometimes I had to try again after I got a more detailed map of the terrain; other times, after I got a rope or some other technical climbing equipment. Every now and then I was missing self-confidence and simply had to take my terror in hand and make myself take the next scary step across an icy gully. (I confess that the peer pressure of 10 other impatient climbers waiting their turn was as motivating as my self-talk.) But I learned that once I figured out what I was missing, I could beg, borrow, improvise, practice, purchase, or regroup. Then I was free to concentrate on moving forward again.

But the main thing I did, and still do, was think small: just concentrate on the next step, the next 12 inches in front of me. It's all I have to master right now. And then the 12 inches after that. And after that. By concentrating on the next step, I've been on top of mountains all over the world. And by concentrating on your next step, you'll find the same technique can work for you. Let's figure out what you are missing so that you can resume your concentration and forward progress.

A BEGIN-ERS CHECKLIST: MISSING LINKS

This is a BEGIN-er's checklist because its purpose is to help you begin. And the way to do that is to identify precisely what you are missing and how to get it. Once you understand what is stopping you, you can develop options. You can fill in your missing links.

Is the reason for your inertia that you are missing one of the following?

- Goals: What is success?
- Resources: Do you have enough people, equipment, or money?
- Time: How much is enough?
- Skill: Do you know how?
- Information: What do you need to know?
- Personal style: Do your work habits need work?

Goals: What Is Success?

Picture success; that is, after you have overcome your procrastination, where will you be? Is that what you want? To answer that question successfully, you have to be a goal setter. And goal setting is tricky because it takes you right back to the "shoulds" and "don't want tos." Goals definitely have an emotional component.

Missing link: You need to set goals. To become a nonprocrastinator, you want to become a good goal setter. The reasons to have clear goals are that goals

Provide focus and keep you on track

Establish your priorities so that you can say no to what is of lesser importance

Narrow your options and provide direction

Define what success will be for you

Reflect your values and force you to think about what is important

Stop right now and ask yourself if the reason you are still procrastinating is that you don't know exactly what outcome you want and what success will be. If you can't provide a quick, firm answer to that question, you need to do your homework and set some goals.

What to do. Learn how. This is not a book on goal setting. If you need help in this area, many wonderful classes and training opportunities are available. Check with your human resources or training department, adult education and community college facility, or professional association. Go to the library or bookstore and look at the many books on goal setting. Each writer's style and approach are different; find a book that appeals to you.

There is no reason not to be a goal setter. Lots of help is available.

CHAPTER FIVE

> **Tip**
>
> *Both your professional life and your personal life will benefit from setting goals. Do the two sets complement each other? If not, that might be your problem. When two sets of goals are in conflict, so are your values.*
>
> *For example, perhaps you are procrastinating on making sales phone calls. If your job requires you to promise something your product can't deliver and you are a very straightforward person, these conflicting values could cause you terrific anxiety and result in procrastination. What can you do? The extremes include finding another job and rethinking your values. Somewhere in between is a middle ground. Can you find it?*

After you have set your goals, tell people what they are when appropriate. Remember that other people are not mind readers. Tell then what is important to you and what you define as success. Ask them what they wish to accomplish too. That way you can make sure you are on the same wavelength.

Write down your goals. Don't be overwhelmed by what that means. Remember that piece of paper with the phone number to look up? Writing your goals may be as simple as adding a phrase to that paper about what you want to accomplish with the phone call. It may be more complex, such as starting your life goal notebook. Writing down what you want is powerful. Do it.

Next steps. For now, think small. Write down the results you envision after you stop procrastinating. See if this goal makes sense and is achievable. If so, get started. If not, spend time today refining your goals so that you convince yourself you are doing the right thing. Be honest with yourself; no one else can think for you.

Tip

Two weeks before your annual performance review is a good time to do goal setting. That way, when you sit down with your boss, you will be prepared to propose any new directions you want to take. If you're self-employed, pick a slow time of the year or a period around New Year's Day.

Confessions of a procrastinator

Barb was recently divorced and was eager to try new things in her life. She had started dating Charles, who wanted to take their relationship to the next level. She was reluctant. He asked her why she was procrastinating, and she was unable to tell him.

Barb's husband had been traditional, and so one thing she liked about the new romance was that Charles was "sensitive" and "open-minded." This new man had been to many personal enrichment classes, and Barb was delighted that he enjoyed discussing feelings and wasn't afraid of intimate conversations.

On their third date she told him that her goal was to live an interesting life. She was astonished to see her date's expression: He was appalled. He quickly told her that that was not a worthy goal and that she needed a more noble calling. The relationship never matured. Later Barb realized that she had every right to set her own goals and that she would live alone until (and when) she found someone who wouldn't judge her. She realized Charles thought interesting meant easy and superficial. But by Barb's standards, Mother Theresa led an interesting life.

Question: Are you procrastinating because you haven't thought through what you want? Are other people unduly influencing what you "should" do?

Tip

Goal setting involves identifying what you want to do more of and what you want to do less of. Get out two pieces of paper, label them accordingly, and start writing.

Confessions of a procrastinator

Lynn had always wanted to run a marathon, but she was 52 years old and had long since concluded that her knees would never take the pounding. One day on a hike she overhead Kathy talking about what fun the Honolulu marathon was. Another hiker asked Kathy how long it took her to finish, and Lynn was astonished to hear her reply, "I try to finish in less than seven hours." Lynn's head swiveled, and the two began a conversation.

The next year Lynn was the proud recipient of a T-shirt and puka bead necklace with a finisher medal on it. Her certificate noted her official time at 7 hours, 37 minutes, 40 seconds. (Kathy and Lynn lost a half hour because of their stop at Burger King.) Lynn rethought her goals: She realized that what she really wanted was to *finish* a marathon, not run one.

Are you procrastinating because your goals need work? If so, get out a pencil and start writing. You are going to have fun meeting this goal and crossing it off your to-do list! And after you complete this long-overdue project, what's next? Be sure to make it fun; you deserve it.

Question: Can your goals be reworked?

Resources: Do You Have Enough People, Equipment, Money?

Completing an activity usually requires resources. Resources include other people, specialized equipment, and money, funds, or a budget. Are you procrastinating because you are missing something? If so, that is your problem.

Missing link. The secret is a two-pronged approach. First you need to identify what you are missing; then you need to find the missing resources. Treat them as two separate steps. Lack of resources is the reason often given for procrastination, but that doesn't have to stop you. Put your energy into how you can make do, not into what you lack. Once you have clearly identified your missing resources, you will be confronted with specific tasks to complete instead of vague anxiety, frustration, and uncertainty.

What to do. Start by making a list of what you need to complete your project. Take a piece of paper, enter the following headings, and then add any more that make sense:

People: If you don't have your own staff, this can be a major stumbling block.

Equipment: Include computers, tools, and supplies.

Money: Do you have enough? Is this project "in the budget"?

Location: Where will you do your work? Do you need someplace special?

Other: What else can you think of? Add things that are stopping you.

This scenario can unfold in several ways. Perhaps you make your list and realize you have access to everything; you just have to go get it or arrange for delivery. If so, that is today's project. By contrast, you may realize you are stuck. You are missing one or more of the above items and don't know what to do.

Now is the time to get creative. Before you give up and abandon your project, ask yourself

What can you borrow, trade for, or rent?

Who owes you a favor?

How can you improvise or make do?

When might your missing items become available?

(List other possibilities here.)

> **Tip**
> *Assume you won't have everything you need at first. That way you don't set yourself up for failure. You begin your project mentally prepared to go on a hunt.*

A special case is lack of organizational support. Sometimes you are unable to complete your project because it is bigger than you. If you work in a large corporation or for the government, the cooperation of many departments and locations can be involved. Any sort of change or special request is complicated. And many times the organization is unable to move as quickly or be as flexible as you would like. This isn't right or wrong; it just is. Therefore, when you are stopped by an obstacle you can't control, put on your thinking cap and look for other routes. Remember, the good news about these large organizations is that they do have an enormous amount of resources. Your challenge is to access them.

> **Tip**
>
> *Very few people or companies have "enough money." Successful people get things done anyway. Being short of money is frequently an excuse, not a real missing link. What you need more of is creative ideas. Look around for someone you admire. How would that person do things?*

Question: If you're short on money, what can you sell? If you are procrastinating because you lack resources, be very specific about what they are. Then go find them—one way or another.

Time: How Much Is Enough?

After money, the second most common shortage is time. There simply aren't enough minutes in the day to get things done, yet some busy people manage. How do they do it? They've learned some tricks, and you can too.

Missing link. You lack time. You have too much to do and not enough time to do it in. You feel frazzled, stressed, and frustrated. How can you break this cycle? Alas, there's no way to manufacture any more minutes per day. You need a different approach, one that gives you the satisfaction of knowing you have used your quota of time wisely and that increases your productivity so that you get more done.

What to do. Managing time is learned behavior. Nobody is born a perfect organizer. Other people improve their time management skills, and so can you. Benefit from other people's expertise and research. As with goal setting, this is not a book on time management, but fabulous books are available. Again, go to the local bookstore or library and skim the chapter titles to find approaches that appeal to you. If your budget permits, good time management

Confessions of a procrastinator

Sam had promised his crew he would remodel the shop and put in some new workbenches. The crew members kept asking him when this would happen, and he kept stalling them. He worked for a small company, and money was tight.

Finally he had a brainstorm. His wife made money with garage sales; why couldn't he do that with all the stuff he and the crew no longer used? He went to his boss for permission. The boss said okay but wait six weeks until it was time to take a physical inventory; that was when they cleaned the shop to prepare for counting the parts. When inventory time came, he and the crew set aside a special shelf where everything unused would go. They gathered obsolete and broken parts, returned equipment that was scrap, broken oscilloscopes, and duplicate hand tools. They also decided they could get by with one fewer file cabinet and table.

The crew all had good ideas. The purchasing agent called surplus shops to see if anything could be sold. He also checked with scrap metal companies to see what could be recycled. Sam proposed to his boss that he sell the office furniture at his wife's garage sale and give her a 10 percent commission. The boss said okay. Another crew member had a friend who bought used motors, and they sold some stuff to him.

All in all they collected $700 for new benches, but Sam wasn't done yet. He then took the Sunday classified ads and looked for workbenches for sale. He found a company that was downsizing and had high-quality items stored in a warehouse a few miles away. He had just enough money to reoutfit the shop and buy pizzas for lunch the day of the remodeling.

books are worth buying because you will refer to them over and over for many years.

People play games with time. Are you procrastinating because

- *You're waiting for the perfect time.* Look to the next few months. When is it going to occur? Two possibilities exist. First, things really will ease up and you can schedule your project then. If so, put it on the calendar and wait. Second, no better time appears. If so, either do it now or abandon it. Which is it going to be?

- *You are so "busy and important."* Test yourself. Have you unconsciously created an acceptable excuse for not beginning? If so, smile at your rather human vanity and get started.

- *You need to tell someone no.* However, you don't quite have the guts, so you keep putting that person off with an "I'm busy." If that is the case, just tell the person no and get it over with. You're exhausting both of you.

- *You don't know how but won't admit it.* I confess this is dear to my heart because it was my trick the first time I had to do a budget. I didn't have a clue how to estimate numbers for the mysterious line items but was reluctant to admit this to my boss. Instead I just kept "being too busy and short of time." He finally forced me to admit what was going on. It was a humiliating moment, but he also helped me get the training I needed.

- *You don't like somebody and are being passive-aggressive with that person.* What a great way to settle an old grudge with a coworker: be "too busy" to help that person just now. However, the project continues to loom. If this describes you, you have two different issues to resolve: the grudge and the present task. Separate them and proceed accordingly.

- *More important things keep coming up.* See the goals section earlier in this chapter.

> **Tip**
>
> *Putting off some things is foolish. For example, if you definitely are going to install a burglar alarm system or purchase a small tool that will make your life easier, spend the time and do it now.*

> **Tip**
>
> *Doing nothing can be a fabulous use of your time. Doing nothing includes the time to sit, to enjoy the present, to recharge your batteries (both physical and psychic), to rest, and to think. Managing your time wisely does not mean always being busy.*

Question: Are you procrastinating because you lack time? If so, take a look at your priorities. Are you doing the most important thing right now? Are you a good time manager? You'll never get any more time. But starting now, you can change how you use what you have.

Skill: Do You Know How?

If you don't know how to do something, it's no wonder you are procrastinating. At an emotional level perhaps you are afraid you'll look dumb, blow it, or humiliate yourself. At a practical level you suspect that the project is going to take a lot of time, time spent fumbling along and being inefficient and ineffective. Finally, perhaps you don't even know where to begin. Your procrastination is so overpowering that you feel like a smooth blank wall is in front of you, one with no handholds or steps. How discouraging.

Even if you have done something before, you may not be very good at it. Being human means that some things you shine at and some things you don't. And it's easy to keep putting off the things you know you're not very good at.

In both cases you lack skill. Lack of skill is a major reason why people procrastinate. And I have good news: This is the easiest obstacle to overcome. All you have to do is learn how. The key word is *learn*.

Missing Link: You need to improve your skills, technique, or knowledge. Becoming better at something can provide enormous rewards. By investing in your own skills bank, you

- *Become faster.* The time it takes is greatly reduced once you learn the proper techniques and procedures.

- *Gain confidence.* The first few times you do anything are always the hardest. You still won't like everything you have to do, but you will become better at it.

- *Do more quality work.* Learning how to do things right has an enormous payoff. It's the way you cross an item off your to-do list once and for all because it doesn't have to be redone.

An alternative: Trial and error. An alternative to improving your skills systematically is to teach yourself through trial and error. This has its pluses and minuses. There is no question your mastery is complete once you have tried many options and figured out what works and what doesn't. When you find a technique that suits you, you will be an expert. Anyone who has ever mastered a computer program knows that eventually you have to do a backup of your work and then sit down and start pushing keys. Theory is nice, but hands-on experience is better.

The question is, When does trial and error make sense? Trial and error is expensive, time-consuming, and inefficient. Also, you may not stumble onto the best way. You may become stuck and give up. You may miss a window of opportunity while you are fiddling around.

The main problem with trial and error is that you lose the benefit of other people's prior efforts. You are "reinventing a wheel" that others have spent a lot of time perfecting. Before considering

CHAPTER FIVE

trial and effort, stop and ask yourself who, if anyone, has faced this situation before and may be able to help you.

One potential stumbling block is that you believe your situation is unique and only you can come up with a solution. You are an extraordinary person, but it is naive to think that you are so unusual that no one else has faced your concerns. Most times you can learn from others. Be aware that while you are fiddling around, other successful people are using that shortcut right now. *Question:* Is your time better spent experimenting with various approaches or researching how to improve your skills?

What to do. Lacking skill is one of the easier missing links to complete. Three things you have to figure out are

- *What you don't know.* This means you write down exactly what you don't know how to do. See if it has a name. Discuss your frustrations and fuzzy thinking with your friends or coworkers; they may be able to give your missing skill a name. For example, they may say, "Joyce, what you don't know how to do is extract key data from the quarterly reports. Let me show you how."

- *Who or what else does know.* Ask yourself where your missing knowledge is located. Possibilities include in-house training programs, community colleges (classes are usually more practical than four-year programs, which concentrate on theory), professional associations, specialized seminars, self-study programs, audiotapes, and public seminars. Written material is another great source, including books, workbooks, pamphlets, and guidelines. People are another source, including bosses, coworkers, team members, and friends. Can you volunteer for a special assignment or committee? Put on your creative thinking cap and start looking around.

> **Tip**
>
> *If you abuse the experts, they will avoid you. Many people are glad to help you out, but you don't want to become a pest. Take yourself as far as you can. Acquire basic knowledge on your own and then ask the expert a more sophisticated question. That way you will be perceived as smart and not as a pest or too lazy to do your own homework. An example of a thoughtful question is something like, "Boss, I've been studying the principles of _____, but I can't make it work with _____ (your specific situation here). Where am I going wrong?"*

- *How you can access the body of knowledge.* The final step is to get schedules and costs, set aside the time, and make learning your missing skills a priority. What a great opportunity to learn something new and become good at something. If you invest your time wisely, the benefits will be lifelong.

Test for missing skills. There are certain times in your life when you suspect that lack of skills is holding you back. See if any of the situations in the following list apply to you.

Be alert for missing skills when you

- *Are completely new to something.* If you have never done something before, assume you don't know how.

- *Are inexperienced.* Have you just gotten a promotion or new job duties or been assigned to a committee? Then you have a lot to learn. For example, if this is the first time you have ever supervised, you may find yourself putting off that first heart-to-heart talk with a nonperforming employee. You don't know exactly what to say or how to say it.

- *Are rusty or out of practice.* Maybe it's been a while since you
  _____. Is that making you reluctant to proceed?

- *Have theory but no hands-on knowledge.* This is a special case for
  all you smart young management trainees and new graduates
  of professional schools. You can write a wonderful paper and
  discuss at great length the theory of what should be done, but
  when it comes to actually making the cut, doing the entry, or
  signing your name to the recommendation, you find yourself
  hesitant. Jump in! You'll learn. Check with your supervisor
  frequently. He or she would far rather catch the mistakes
  when they're little ones.

Question: What difficult task are you avoiding because you lack
skill?

Tip

*Some skills aren't worth learning. If you hate to do
something, other people can do it cheaper and better, or the task doesn't come up very often, think
twice about increasing your skill. You may be better
off hiring, delegating, or contracting out the work.*

The role of mastery. Acquiring skill can take a lot of time and
commitment. Pick one or two things to be really good at. Establish
your reputation as the expert on those things. For everything else,
stop and ask yourself whether increasing your skill makes sense.
For example, are you going to improve your skills at computer soli-
taire or spreadsheets? You will come up with different answers for
each situation. But you will definitely procrastinate less once you
choose what to be good at.

Confessions of a procrastinator

Jere was the new regional sales manager, and he was excited. He had lots of good ideas and knew he could increase profits. While he was writing his business plan, Wally, one of his direct reports, asked for a meeting. As they sat down, Wally explained that he had been doing inside sales (telephone support) for the last two years and was ready to hit the road and be an outside salesperson. He was experienced and eager, and his wife was supportive of the travel. That was where the money was, and he wanted it.

Jere was caught by surprise and said he would think about it. The problem was that Wally had body odor, which wasn't a problem as long as he stayed in his own cubicle. But the company required more professionalism for calling on customers. Jere realized he was avoiding Wally because he didn't know what to say or how to say it. He lacked skill in having this type of heart-to-heart talk.

Jere did two things: he invited the most experienced supervisor in the company to coffee and picked her brain, and he called up a buddy in his professional association for tips. He then drafted an outline of what he had to tell Wally. He stumbled a bit during the conversation, but he leveled with him. Wally's face flushed, but the next day he didn't stink. Wally became the highest producing salesperson in the department, and Jere got the reputation of being an honest, supportive supervisor whose people stuck by him.

Information: What Do You Need to Know?

Do you need more information? Or are you procrastinating? The line between the two is subtle. The role of information in decision making is discussed more fully in Part II. For now, I just want you to challenge yourself and your assumptions. Information is like time. Nobody ever has enough, but some people manage anyway.

Missing Link: You want better information. Information is the raw material of every decision you make, and as such it is very powerful. More information can lead to better decisions, but not always. Have you ever been overwhelmed by piles of computer printouts on your desk? You procrastinate because you are simply unable to face them, too overwhelmed to dig out what you need to know to go forward. Improving the quality of your information will improve the quality of your decisions. Just as in cooking, the better the ingredients, the better the finished dish. However, just as in cooking, some nights scrambled eggs with leftovers stirred in and stale bread made into toast are good enough.

Managing information is an art and a balancing act. You want to

Get enough information but not more than you can use.

Acquire good data but not miss an opportunity when partial information would have been good enough.

Trust your research without acquiring details that don't add much.

What to do. When you find yourself at a standstill because of information, three possibilities exist. Ask yourself whether you have too much, too little, or inaccurate information.

Too much information. If you have too much information, your challenge is to ferret out the key points.

To do that, you can

Use a summary or executive report. Does one already exist? Can one of your coworkers create it?

Sort the data by table of contents, headings, or index. Then look only at the parts that are essential to your project.

Use only the most recent data.

Do some sort of spot check or sample.

Skim the information, looking for key words with a colored pencil. Then go back and read those parts only.

Decide how much research time the information is worth, for example, two hours. Then either review it all at once or review it for 15 minutes a day until that two hours is spent. Then stop gathering and use what you know.

Too little information. Are you stuck because you are missing key material? If so, ask yourself

Whether the information exists at all. If it does, how can you get to it?

If no information exists, is it realistic to create it? Cost-effective? Timely?

Whether you can make do with the partial material you have now.

If other people have more material than you do, will they share it?

If it is possible to make progress knowing only what you know now. If so, go ahead.

Inaccurate, incomplete, or poor information. Is your missing link that you don't trust what you have? Here are some steps you can take. Ask yourself if

A more reliable source is available. If so, can you get to it? Perhaps it's a sunny Saturday and you want to go car shopping. But you decide to go to the library and do car research instead so that you will be less vulnerable to unrealistic promises and undocumented claims.

Your personal knowledge can be used instead. Sometimes "good enough" is.

Risking a poor result will be serious, expensive, or difficult to change. For example, does your project involve a safety issue or put human life at risk? If so, don't order the parts until you are certain they meet your specifications.

Just a bit of refining will greatly increase the usefulness of what you have. For example, assume you are preparing a budget. If it would take you one hour to get accurate totals of your expenses, do it. The return on investment is in your favor.

Give up your fact fantasies.   The reality is that most of the information you use to make decisions is not facts. The purest definition of a fact is something you can verify with your five senses. It is a fact to me when "I heard you say that" or "I saw you there." But most of your day is spent dealing with missing, confusing, and unclear opinions; filtered summaries; memories; and estimates and projections. Prepare yourself right now to begin moving in the world of conflicting, complex information. Decide what you need to know, get it, and move on. If you are waiting to get all the facts, you will miss opportunities.

The role of fear.   Examine closely your assumption that information is holding you up. Are you really

Afraid you'll make a mistake?

Looking for a guarantee that whatever you decide will be right?

Preparing to justify your actions in case things don't go the way you hope?

If so, ask yourself whether information can lay these fears to rest. If necessary, reread the previous chapter, "Success Means Entering the Risk Zone." Then proceed accordingly.

Tip

Knowledge is cumulative. You will know more tomorrow than you do today. If waiting makes sense and will increase your knowledge base, do it. But be aware that waiting can cost you an opportunity, a door might close, or a competitor might beat you.

If you decide to go ahead and you make a mistake, shrug your shoulders and tell yourself that you did the best you could with the information you had at the time. Life is one continuous learning experience.

Next steps.   Give up any fantasy that you can know it all. Write down exactly what you want to know, where you can find it, and how long the research will take you. Take a hard look at your list. Either revise it and get more realistic or get going. Either way, you have work to do.

Question: Are you procrastinating because your assumptions about information are unrealistic?

Personal Style: Do Your Work Habits Need Work?

Is it possible that your problem is you? To be more precise, are you procrastinating because of your personal style? If you are wiggling uncomfortably, keep reading. These tips may be just what you need to jump-start yourself.

Missing Link: You need to let go of old habits.   Some things at work and in life aren't very much fun, but you do them anyway. That's what self-discipline is. The good news is that the dread is usually more unpleasant and lasts longer than just doing the deed.

Your challenge is to find ways to move yourself forward when the desire just isn't there. It can be done, and the good news is that when you do it, an enormous weight will fall off your shoulders. You'll free up tremendous mental and physical energy and be ready to tackle those interesting new projects that your guilt would not permit you to start.

What to do.   Accept the fact that there are many ways to get things done. If you are stuck, a different approach may be just what you need.

Psychologists have come up with many useful classifications of personality types, and it is not my intention to duplicate them here. I am assuming that you are proud of your own strengths and painfully aware of your weaknesses. Your challenge is to take that self-knowledge and use it to work through your reluctance to take action.

Ask yourself: Do I need to do more of something or less of something? Being out of balance in either direction reduces your chance for success. If you are a perfectionist, maybe you need to ease up on the details and on yourself. Challenge yourself to recognize "good enough" and stop there.

If you are a dreamer, a global thinker, maybe you need to finish what you start and pay attention to the details. If you don't, not much will happen and you may gain the reputation of being a big talker but not much of a finisher.

In short, no matter what your approach is, it's good, but not perfect. Cherish your strengths, accept your limitations, and figure out how to work around them. Seek feedback; people will be happy to give it to you.

> *Tip*
> *Remind yourself that there are many things in life you don't have to like. You just have to do them.*

Question: Who balances your personal style?

Confessions of a procrastinator

I am in the business of designing, manufacturing, and distributing ultrasonic fish finders and sonars with my husband, Nathan Roundy. Nathan is an inventor, which means he looks normal but his view of things is very "interesting." Our approaches are different. I am a worrier, planner, and thinker. I try to anticipate everything that might go wrong and prepare for it. Nathan is an optimist, dreamer, and creative thinker. He starts having fun when things fall apart.

On our first hike together many years ago a wild rainstorm came up. We opened our backpacks and started giggling in the downpour when we saw our differences illustrated. He had one pair of wool mittens with the fingertips missing. I had five pair of hand coverings, including glove liners, waterproof overmitts, spare glove liners, a pair of socks that could cover my hands in a pinch, and rubber gloves for medical emergencies. When I accused him of being a "half-mitt," he reminded me that I was a "five-mitt." I was well prepared, but my pack was so heavy that I couldn't cover the miles very fast. He had the bare minimum but could quickly hike out of a difficult situation if he had to.

After our amusement subsided, we realized we made a good team. I am well prepared but not always flexible. I have to be pushed to try new things. Nathan is rather "casual" (his word, not mine) in his approach. Details aren't his strong suit. But he has vision; the mundane does not constrain him. He sees what things could become and can move really fast when necessary.

> **Tip**
>
> *People who exasperate you probably have perspectives you lack. Take a minute and concentrate on a coworker you find annoying. Ask yourself exactly why that person gets to you. Tell yourself that you can learn from that person's comments, questions, and objections. These people aren't picking on you personally; they have perspectives you can use, and listening to their concerns can save you from making painful mistakes.*

Next step. For a week or so observe yourself and others. Zero in on people you find effective. When you find yourself stuck, imagine what they would do and try that.

> **Remember**
>
> Overcoming inertia requires you to identifly very specifically why you are stuck. The questions here include: Are your goals clear? Do you have enough resources? Have you scheduled your time? Are your skills good enough? Is your information sufficient? Is your personal style holding you back?
>
> Pinpoint the nature of your reluctance and you will be well along the way to overcoming it. Procrastinate no more! Get your task done and move on to your hour of joy.

SUCCESS—CONGRATULATIONS!

This chapter opened with a question: Are you stuck? After working through your BEGIN-er's checklist, you know what to do and you're ready to do it.

When you have succeeded in breaking the cycle of procrastination, you will feel a strong sense of accomplishment. You did it! You should feel proud of yourself.

At the same time, please don't be discouraged if you slip occasionally. We all do. Just get out this book and give yourself a refresher course. You'll be pleased at how much faster you catch yourself and break the cycle the next time.

Look up at your horizons. Do you see bright skies and broad reaches? Those clouds holding boring old guilt trips have blown away. You know that you'll still have an occasional storm but that it too will pass.

Go forth and live an interesting life. Enjoy the sparkle in the minutes flowing through your life timer. Look for new and different hours of joy to experience. Grow. Promote yourself to the next level: situations in which you don't know what to do. How exciting! Adventure awaits. Turn the page and start Part II.

PART II
RESOLUTION

Are you a procrastinator?

Maybe not. If you don't take action because you don't know what to do, you are not a procrastinator. You are a thinker, a person with a situation to resolve.

Add the word *thinker* to your self-description right now. If you are reading this book, you are a thinker. Why not be a good one? The payoff is enormous because you use your mind to make choices all day long. You will have fun once you realize that thinking is part of the game of life and you are a worthy competitor. Increasing your thinking skills is the secret to making your plans work out, your dreams come true, and your world expand.

Uncertainty can be very stressful and anxiety-producing, but figuring out what to do and doing it constiutes one of the most satisfying parts of life. Once you know you can make your own decisions, put them in place, and accept the consequences of your choices, you build a center of confidence in yourself that no one can ever take away.

Are your decisions perfect? Of course not; you are a work in progress. But mistakes point you in new directions; they are not dead ends. Is your life full and rich? You bet, and you are eager to see what tomorrow brings because you know whether it's a day filled with ups or downs, you can cope. You survive, and you thrive.

Part II of this book, the seven-step RESOLVE It! decision-making system, will show you how to figure out what to do, beginning with where to start and ending with answers or closure. Note that resolution doesn't mean that your results will be perfect, easy to achieve, or always satisfying. It just means that you will find a solution that is workable for you.

RESOLVE stands for

R: Resolve something

E: Examine what you already know

S: Step into the future

O: Overcome the subtle factors

L: Leap, lurch, or launch into action

V: View and evaluate your results

E: Enjoy your success or learn from experience and then move on

Time is passing. Choices await you. If you know what to do, stop procrastinating and do it. If you don't know what to do, RESOLVE It!

6 R: RESOLVE SOMETHING!

What are you going to do about

- The computer system that needs to be upgraded?
- The expansion that looks promising?
- A project that is trouble?
- The competitor that is gaining?
- Products that needs to be updated?
- The staff shortage?
- Poor cash flow?
- The old car?
- Your teenager who is "acting out"?
- That report that isn't finished?
- The IRA investment you're afraid to make?
- The unprofitable operation?
- Choosing a health insurance plan?
- A person who isn't performing his or her job satisfactorily?
- Whatever has you in a quandary?
- What you can't even say aloud that has you worried sick?

CHAPTER SIX

If you are undecided, uncertain, reluctant, or confused, you have some thinking to do and some decisions to make. Take heart. Help is at hand. This chapter will show you precisely how to get started. You are going to walk along a path of discovery, emerging confident that you have uncovered what is right for you and your situation.

THE "SHOULDS"

You are ready to begin. You want to stop procrastinating and take action. You know what you *should* do. You should

- Get the facts, which will be clear, straightforward, and easy to obtain.
- Make a decision, which will be obvious based on the facts.
- Enjoy good results always.
- Live happily ever; life is sweet as you hum "tra la la" while chasing moonbeams.

But somehow the process doesn't work that way for you.
Instead

- Facts are contradictory, missing, incomplete, and too expensive to gather. And even with the facts you are still confused.
- The decision is not obvious or is unappealing. Perhaps your choices make your gut hurt and you dread the uproar your decision will cause.
- Sometimes your results are good, sometimes not.
- Life has its ups and downs; some days you eat the bear, some days the bear eats you.

The result is that you:

- Enroll in "3 a.m. university," which means you lay awake for two hours in the middle of the night worrying about what to do.

- Do nothing and hate yourself.
- Delay action until most of your options disappear and you do what's left.
- Miss an opportunity because someone else beat you to it.
- Don't even try.
- Panic and make a poor choice.
- Spend enormous amounts of time going over the same decisions.
- Add your own particular pattern here.

After all this, you still don't know what to do or aren't happy with what you did. Sometimes nothing looks good, everything looks good, or the choices are confusing. For most people making a decision feels like being bombarded. Facts, emotions, fears, options, values, beliefs, hopes, constraints, dreams, and possibilities are all jumbled in the mind. What might happen, what did happen, and what could happen form the "chaos of the undifferentiated." Everything is a blur. What are you going to do? You can't decide.

If your decisions aren't perfect, welcome to the human race. And if you're beating yourself up because you don't behave like a model decision maker, guess what! You've fallen victim to "the shoulds" again. Logical, orderly, neat, and tidy left-brain decision making is a myth. The world is complicated, and so is figuring out what to do. But there is a better way than tossing and turning at 3 a.m., which wrecks your sleep and your hair and doesn't do much for your decision making either. And that is to RESOLVE It!

DECISION MAKING DEFINED

It's time for definitions. Decision making is the act of making a choice that ends uncertainty. Thinking is the process of using your mind to explore your choices and come to conclusions. Throughout this book I will use the terms *thinking* and *decision*

"Be nice, dear." Those are the words I was raised by, typical advice for a girl growing up in Kent, Ohio, in the 1950s and 1960s. And I quickly learned that "be nice" meant "be no trouble." But there is a price to pay for being nice: Nice means you have to do what other people want you to do. And being nice was killing me, as I learned when I got high blood pressure at age 32 from trying so hard to please everyone else. Fortunately I stumbled upon a wise physician who told me to quit smoking, lose weight, start jogging, and generally shape up my lifestyle long before it was fashionable to do so.

Since being nice was hazardous to my health, I decided to take on some real risk and climb Mount Rainier in Washington state. At 14,410 feet, the peak is the most glaciated in the mainland United States. It is a technical climb requiring ice ax, crampons, and ropes but mostly requiring stamina. Climbing consists of hour after hour of putting one foot in front of the other in treacherous conditions of steep, slippery ice and deep, tiring snow. The total elevation gain is nearly 10,000 feet; imagine climbing up a ladder for two miles. I signed up with the guide service, paid my money, and reached the summit. And it changed my life.

I learned I could have severe abdominal cramps that doubled me over and still take one more step, that I could be filled with absolute terror and not quit, that I could be altitude sick and still gag down food for fuel. But I learned a far more important lesson that changed me forever: Life was quite interesting when I asked myself what I wanted to do and did it.

(continued)

Thinking for yourself extracts a price. Some people don't like you as much. There's no one else to blame. Role models and easy answers are hard to find; you have to chart your own path. You have to take care of yourself, house-sitting, living on unemployment, and buying day-old bread when things are tough. But not thinking for yourself extracts a far higher price: your soul, your potential, your sparkle, your gifts to the world.

Can you be nice and be a thinker at the same time? I doubt it. You can be kind, generous, loving, warm, and affectionate. But give up nice. Instead be independent, capable, and interesting.

making, and *thinker* and *decision maker* interchangeably. Call yourself whatever term appeals to you or make up your own term.

The decision-making process begins when you first become aware that a situation is changing and ends when you evaluate the success or failure of your efforts. But decision making never really goes away; you just move along to something new. Throughout your life you are continuously faced with making new decisions.

DECISION MAKING: A SKILL THAT IMPROVES WITH PRACTICE AND GOOD TECHNIQUE

Have you ever had any training in decision-making and thinking skills? Few people have. My reason for writing this book is to provide a model for what I believe is a core human competency that has been neglected by schools, universities, adult education providers, and corporate training programs. As with any skill, thinking can be improved with practice and good technique.

None of us were born knowing how to think; it is learned behavior. Take a minute and reflect on the training you have received so far. If you are lucky, you had parents who deliberately let you make up your own mind as a child, helping you explore your options and the consequences of your actions. If you are lucky, you had mentors—wise, experienced people who encouraged you and kindly told you in private where you were going wrong and what subtle clues you were missing. Perhaps you were part of a management training or executive development program. Maybe you were a military officer. Then again, if you are like most people, you had none of those things. Perhaps you come from what is politely known as a "dysfunctional family" and your boss's idea of leadership is to hide in his or her office, hoping problems will go away. That's okay. You've had other life experiences that have formed your knowledge and character base and that you can use to your advantage. Everybody has something to learn. You are strong, capable, literate, and eager to grow. Only a closed mind can hurt you. And if you had that, you would have put this book down many pages ago.

Tip
Select a role model or mentor now, either real or imaginary. Who do you know and/or admire who is a good decision maker? Look around the office. Ask yourself who comes out on top a lot. Can you take that person to lunch? Great if you can. If not, watch that person closely and see what he or she does and how he or she does it. Then ask yourself how that person would handle your situation. Or pick a literary, fictional, or famous figure for a mentor. These conversations are great because you get to do all the talking.

Many people nowadays have been trained in "teamwork," but to be successful a team must consist of competent individuals who first think for themselves. Otherwise one of two things often happens. The first is that the team is composed of human parrots who imitate the dominant talker because they are too intimidated to speak up or lack their own opinions. The second is that the team is composed of a group of people who don't say much of anything but say it nicely. Neither team is likely to enjoy rousing workplace success. So even when you are working as part of a team, improving your thinking skills is one of the best investments you can make in yourself and your group's success.

YOUR GOAL: RESOLVE SOMETHING

When you are faced with a situation that requires you to make a choice, your goal is to resolve it by making a wise one. Keep in mind, however, that resolution is something you work toward; it is a process, not magic, a miracle, or a shortcut. If the answers were obvious or simple, the procrastination tips in Part I of this book would have gotten you going.

More likely you are stuck. But the good news is that you can use the suggestions in this book to focus your thinking in ways you haven't even anticipated. Let go of your preconceptions about what to do right now. Know that resolution is possible. But accept that you don't know where the process is going to take you. You are a thinker; you are going to open your mind so that you can recognize solutions as they present themselves. What possibilities exist when you begin with an open mind!

THE POWER OF "SORTS"

Sorting is a form of thinking. It is a way to bring order to the chaos that has you overwhelmed. By sorting, you will be able to organize and see patterns in your past, present, and future. You will be able to group options, preferences, and subtleties. In short, sorting is a way to figure out what to do.

The RESOLVE It! system will show you exactly how to sort. After the sorting and sequencing are done, responsibility shifts back to you, for only you can decide what you will do. You have the answers, and sorting will help them appear for you, although it may not make them any more appealing or easy.

The first step of the RESOLVE It! model is R which stands for "resolve one thing, anything, something." Granted, all your situations are important and you will get to all of them sooner or later. But the reality is that you can't do everything at once. You have to pick a place to start.

The rest of this chapter provides the details on how to make the following sorts. To begin, what you have to do is

Sort I:	Identify your difficult situations (gut-wrenchers)
Sort II:	Seek perspective
Sort III:	Turn gut-wrenchers into projects
Sort IV:	Marshal your resolve and pick one

Do these actions sound easy? Yes. Can you do them? Yes. Will you? Ah, there is the catch. Set aside your excuses, including how busy you are, how hopeless things appear, and how you already know everything. Open your mind. Give this system a try. You have nothing to lose but your stomach pains and the circles under your eyes.

Sort I: Identify Your Gut-Wrenchers

First, you want to raise your situations to a conscious level. Denial is exhausting and unproductive. Quit trying to push things to the back of your mind and telling yourself, "I'm being silly; it doesn't matter." It's time to get things out in the open where you can sort through them.

Gut-wrenchers are a good place to focus your initial efforts. I'm sure you know what I mean by *gut-wrenchers*. It's a term I invented to describe tough choices and difficult situations that cause your stomach to go into knots, the kind of agonies that have made antacid manufacturers rich. Gut-wrenchers include more than just unpleasant decisions. Even choosing between two wonderful opportunities can be stressful. Also, minor situations such as the annoying habits of a coworker can tie you in knots.

Here's what to do.

Assemble your tools. Put down this book right now and go get the following:

- A yellow writing tablet or several sheets of scrap paper
- Fifteen file folders (new or used)
- A pencil with an eraser (mistakes are encouraged)

This first exercise won't take very long, and if you do it now, by the time you come to the end of this chapter you will have begun the process of resolving your gut-wrenchers. Just think how good you will feel as the feelings of frustration, hopelessness, and anxiety are replaced with determination and focus.

Do a brain dump. Take your piece of paper and label it across the top: "My Gut-Wrenchers." Write down today's date. Now do a "brain dump." That means you write down every single thing that is worrying you, entering one item per line. This brain dump is for your eyes only, so be brutally honest. You will learn how to sort and prioritize later; for now the important thing is to get those gut-wrenchers onto one sheet of paper in a list format. There is no right or wrong number to write down. Depending on how your life is going at the moment, your list can range from one to a hundred items. Include personal and professional situations. It is not appropriate to resolve personal problems on your employer's nickel, but it is appropriate to clear your brain so that you can concentrate on what you are paid to do.

Here is an example of a list to inspire you:

My Gut-Wrenchers, June 1

The quality of that last batch of circuit boards stinks.

My boss is acting weird. Wonder if I'm in trouble.

I think Brooke is mad at me. What did I do this time?

I haven't heard whether the loan is approved; the suspense is killing me.

Sometimes my car makes a weird (expensive?) noise.

Mom wants me to come home for Thanksgiving. Can I stand it?

Sales of item A are so good that we can't fill orders.

Sales of item B are below projections. What's wrong?

I wasn't included on the new project team.

My significant other forgot my birthday, the rat.

My performance review is coming up. Wonder if she'll mention the budget overruns.

My project is going well and I'd like to do something new, but what?

My boss is retiring. Do I want the job?

Okay, now jot down your own list. It doesn't have to be perfect, neat, coherent, or grammatically correct. What it does have to do is transfer what is whirling around in your brain to paper so that you can think more clearly. Start writing!

Brain dump = your world.   Take a look at your list, for it represents what is important to you. The common framework for those diverse items is that they all involve some sort of situation. Situations can be good ones, such as opportunities; painful ones, such as dilemmas; or challenging ones in which many complex factors are in play. You make decisions about many types of situations all day long. *Situation* is a neutral term. It simply describes a condition, a set of circumstances, that requires you to make a choice.

This chapter focuses on gut-wrenchers because they are the situations that involve worry. Worry is the anticipation—the fear—that things will not turn out as you would like. One reason you worry is that you feel powerless. If you had a magic wand, you could make everything just the way you wanted it, but you don't. However, you can diminish the tremendous emotional energy drain of worry by taking action. Philosophers can't agree on how much control we mere humans have over a situation. But doing *something* will help you worry less because you will have ceased to be passive. For better or worse, you are taking charge, or at least think you are. Either way you feel better.

Shortly you will learn how to organize your list. But for now, just take a minute and review it. What common themes do you see? Do you have many situations or one situation with many pieces? Are your problems related to people, money, systems, or things? Have you included some opportunities? You can tell a lot about yourself by doing a brain dump. Learn what you can and laugh ruefully if it helps.

Sort II: Seek Perspective

Take a look at your list of gut-wrenchers and situations to resolve. Your challenge is to rank-order your situations and pick one to concentrate on. This sort will help you do just that.

Concentrate where it counts. Not only do you want to concentrate where it counts, you want to put your effort where it can do some good. Remember Don Quixote tilting at windmills? Cervantes's classic tale made for great high school reading, but one point of that story was how futile his efforts to subdue the windmills were. For one thing, no matter what he did, the wind just kept blowing; for another, nothing was personal. Some things were just bigger than he was.

You are now going to ask yourself some hard questions. You want to make sure you have not lost perspective or are "tilting at windmills." Here are some questions to ask yourself as you review your list.

- *Is your situation bigger than you?* Realistically, can you do anything about your situation? There are many things that you cannot directly control, including governmental rules, new laws, economic changes, wars, recessions, and natural disasters. You can influence such macrosituations, for example, by writing letters, lobbying, or running for political office, but is that realistic? You have a job to do and need money to support yourself. Take a hard look at your situation. Make a decision right now. Are you going to accept that a situation is bigger than you and cross it off your gut-wrencher list? Or are you going to take it on as a cause? Either answer can be the right one. Just make your choice consciously.

  For example, Mary is a nurse who is really good at comforting people and explaining what is going on to them. But her job has changed to reflect the realities of managed care. She is now much more of an administrator and coordinator, filling out reports and holding meetings. She thinks about changing professions because she misses the good old days. She has a friend she admires who has become a patient advocate and is trying to change the system. Mary admires her but realizes that that path is not for her. She finally decides to let go of her anger at a situation that isn't personal, to sit tight for now and see how things unfold. She'll concentrate on keeping her skills current and review the situation again in a year.

- *Is your situation an exception?* Is your situation a one-time exception that you are better off forgetting about or a trend that needs to be addressed? Everyone makes mistakes, has bad days, and makes poor decisions. When you uncover such situations, your time may be best spent just shrugging them off. Life goes on. Lighten up and put the exceptions into perspective.

- *Is your situation trivial?* Is the outcome important to you? You can't resolve everything. You have lots to do with your life. Spend your time on what is worth the effort.

- *Can you resolve this issue with a minor effort?* If that is all that is needed, go ahead and make the phone call or schedule the meeting. For example, if your boss is acting weird and you don't know why, all you have to do is say to your boss, "I feel like you're a little stressed out. Is there any way I can help you or anything you want me to do differently?" Then you'll know and be able to move on.

- *Is this situation time-sensitive?* This is a variation of the classic time management principle that some things will go away on their own if they are left alone. Look at what you have written. Can you put this on the back burner, or do you need to resolve it now?

Tip

Take a minute and call to awareness the three best decisions you ever made. What can you learn from them? Similarly, pull up the worst ones. What part of the process do you not want to repeat? Learn from your own experiences. You are a great teacher. For example, after completing this exercise Sam realized that his best decisions all involved taking a chance. After realizing this, he resolved to apply for that new job. He might not get it, but he could handle that. Besides, he might be selected!

Charlie was in the fishing industry, and he could see it changing. Fish stocks in the ocean were diminishing because of overfishing. Governments all over the world were setting quotas for how many fish could be caught without doing long-term harm to the resource. A licensing system with expensive permits for fishing vessels was becoming common, and that meant fewer people were buying boats and entering the business. As a supplier of radar, Charlie was in a quandary. His sales were declining, along with the industry.

Charlie was upset. He firmly believed that with certain exceptions overfishing was not happening and that the real problem was that fish stocks were not being assessed accurately. He seriously considered developing a proposal to show how more accurate counting would permit more fishing, thus keeping prices down and food plentiful around the world. He actually drafted a letter to his congresswoman.

Then Charlie took a deep breath and looked at his situation. He was one person with no particular political or policy aspirations. This was a big, complex issue involving governments all over the world and many experts who couldn't agree. He had a family to feed and retirement to save for. Charlie decided to let go of this issue and instead expand his market and sell his product to yachts and pleasure boats. He still thought he was right about overfishing but contented himself with occasionally expounding at an industry cocktail party.

Now review your list of gut-wrenchers. Cross off any situations that no longer interest you and add ones if necessary. For now, combine all situations that have a common thread into one project. Recopy your notes with more focus and clarity. Rephrase if necessary. Mentally answer the question: "I don't know what to do about the _____ situation," and let your answers form your revised list.

Sort III: Turn Gut-Wrenchers into Projects

Your feelings of being overwhelmed should subside and your sense of power and confidence should increase as you get perspective on the situation. It's time for a mind shift. Here are some techniques to help you move forward.

Go neutral. The next step is to turn your list of gut-wrenchers into projects. This is a powerful concept because you are now going to give up the term *gut-wrencher* and the lack of control it implies. Instead you are going to pick neutral names that simply describe your situation. From here on in you have projects to do. Exaggerating for effect is fun and a way to admit your fear, but you're in charge now, and it's time for your language to reflect it. For example, the item on your list "Sue incompetent circuit board house," now becomes "Review circuit board status."

Create project folders. Now take your file folders and label them with the names of your situations. You can have one file or a hundred. Any number is okay. Ten is a good number; you'll see why in a minute. Create a final folder labeled "Stuff to Do Someday" and toss your leftover gut-wrenchers into that folder.

You should be feeling better now. Look what you have done: You have performed a "brain dump" so that thoughts are no longer swirling around, causing stress, sleeplessness, and distraction. You have let go of the emotional language that made you feel powerless. You have turned your situations into projects complete with folders. And this chapter has still more tips, so you aren't done yet.

There is hope. Things will work out. Correction: *You* are going to work things out. Better still: You *are* working things out.

Tip
Resolve one situation per month. If your list has 10 situations, a reasonable number, you can resolve one situation a month with December off for the holidays and July or August off for vacation. If your list has fewer than 10 items, great. You can add more as they come up. If your number is greater than 10, be careful. You may have unrealistic expectations for yourself and what you can get done. Take another look at the list and see what you can let slip, ignore, or live with.

Fill your project folders.   The final step is to assemble any and all relevant information collected to date into one place: your project folder. If the folder is blank, add anything that comes up. If your information is scattered, gather the articles, forms, reports, notes, and outlines—in short, anything you have accumulated that will help you put this situation in one place: the folder.

Tip
If your project requires more than a folder, identify a shelf, file drawer, or box that can hold everything. The main thing is to cluster all related information.

Sort IV: Marshal Your Resolve and Pick One

Sequence your projects.   Take a look at your folders. Put them in some sort of order. One possibility is by due dates. For example, the federal income tax due date is April. A fiscal year close might be December 31. Another possibility is to classify by what is most important. Play with and shuffle your folders, looking for a sequence that makes sense and is workable.

> *Tip:*
> *Assign each folder a review month. Start a project two or three months before it is due. Begin long-term projects during slow months. Yes, your life is always crazy, but some months are worse than others, such as when a fiscal year is closing or when you have a seasonal rush. For example, your income tax folder could be started in February after the December bank statements are in but before it is too late to get any missing information.*

Pick one. Review your projects and put the folder that represents the situation you are going to resolve first on your desk.

Are you stuck? You still can't decide what situation to resolve first? Then take all your folders and shuffle them as if you were playing cards. Cut the deck in half. The one that's on top is it! Begin with that.

Schedule time to begin. Get out your calendar and schedule a one-hour "lunch with Lynn" (or anything else you want to call it) in the next week or so. What you are doing is establishing a time to think things through, a time to organize your thoughts, plan, schedule, review, dream, and evaluate. One hour is more than enough. The secret is to do only one thing at a time. You'll be amazed at how much you accomplish. You may even finish early.

Unless you have a very unusual workplace, it is almost impossible to think at your desk. You may be able to find an unused conference room, hidden stairwell, or empty office. Perhaps you can leave the building. If you try to work in the employee cafeteria, you probably will be interrupted. After all, you're "not busy." You're only thinking, right? Clear your absence with your boss if necessary. Go ahead and ask; he or she probably will be delighted with your resolve. You are becoming the kind of person who gets raises and more than his or her share of the incentive pools.

Remember

Decision making is a skill that improves with practice and good technique. It is also a messy process that takes time. A series of "sorts" is the key to helping you bring order to chaos. The first step is to do a brain dump to bring all those swirling thoughts to a conscious level. The next step is to seek perspective. Finally, turn those decisions into projects complete with files. Pick one project to resolve and begin with that. Put the rest of your folders away until their time comes up.

Let your worries slide into proper perspective: a part of your life but not overwhelming. What can you do right now to enjoy *this* moment and make the most of it? Go out and savor an hour of joy; you've earned it.

That's it for now. Set aside your project folders until your "lunch with Lynn." What's on the menu for lunch? Turn to Chapter 7 and find out.

7 E: EXAMINE WHAT YOU ALREADY KNOW

THE REALITY OF THE PAST

What brought you to where you are now? Why does your gut hurt? What were the causes and contributing factors? Probably many things have contributed to your uncertainty. Money (perhaps too much) has been spent. Time (some of it lost) has been invested. Perhaps feelings (including yours) have been hurt. Your situation has a history, and denying what has brought you to the spot you are in now represents a failure to face reality. The past simply is, and as a good decision maker you want to learn what you can, set aside what doesn't matter, and forgive yourself for your mistakes. Time is moving on, and you want to move on too.

The past is unlikely to repeat itself exactly the same way, and so your purpose is not to rehash the conversation that didn't go well or to beat yourself up over what you did or didn't do. Instead, what you are going to do over lunch today is look back and learn what you can from the past. Your scope of thinking is from whenever your situation became in need of change to the present.

Chapter 8 will take you into the future, but for now let it go. For one thing, it hasn't happened yet. Your past has, and so today you are going to concentrate on realities, not on possibilities. But let me warn you right now that this is not a neat, orderly, perfect process. Decision making is messy.

Your goals for today's "lunch" are to

Confirm your certainty about what has happened to date

Look for patterns and trends that point to future probabilities

Realistically assess where you are right now

Document your actions (if that becomes necessary)

Prepare a list for what to do next

See if a solution or plan of action jumps out at you

It's time to get started. Where are you sitting—an empty office, a coffee shop, a library, a picnic table? Any place will work as long as you have your folders, calendar, and supplies (pencil and paper) and are away from interruptions.

TAP YOUR POWER OF CONCENTRATION

Resolution takes concentration, so you want to be ready to concentrate. Do you know what concentration looks like and feels like? When you are concentrating, you often appear to be frowning. Your brow is furrowed, and you are somewhat oblivious to what is going on. You appear preoccupied and possibly stern. If people come by who are used to seeing you with a "happy" social face, you may have to notify them of the change. Otherwise they may take it personally and think you are mad at them. All you need to do is indicate in a diplomatic way that you're working on something and don't want to be interrupted. Just look them in the eye and let your determination show.

A FRESH PERSPECTIVE: MULL, DON'T JUDGE

There are two types of thinking: mulling and judging. Mulling is the process of suspending judgment. Instead of judging, you note what is, what was, what could be, and what might be. You observe and let your mind float. Judgment is the process of applying merit. You'll be doing that in future chapters, but for today use mind-sets out of the mulling column. Otherwise you are narrowing your options too soon.

Mulling Phrases	Judgment Phrases
That's noteworthy	That's good/bad
What a surprise	I/you are right or wrong
How interesting	This is disgusting, bad, great, good
I didn't know that	This will/won't work
I wonder what else—	I/you are stupid, smart, wrong, right
Is that possible?	There's no chance; this is perfect

Feel free to add your own. In fact, try to catch yourself using judgmental phrases inappropriately. Such language influences your behavior and can cause you to make poor decisions. You literally talk yourself into it!

> Allison loved being the center of attention and was quite dramatic in her style. But as she told me, "I finally realized I was taking my theatrical flair too far. It was hurting my ability to make good decisions because I tended to overstate everything. For example, my boss failed to call me back today by the appointed time; in my words, he 'was a complete bozo who couldn't tell time with a grandfather clock.' I finally realized that not only were my statements not true and often unkind, they were causing me to overreact and get upset unnecessarily. My personal challenge for myself is to describe situations literally. I know it's a lesson that will serve me well."

CHAPTER SEVEN

INFORMATION: THE RAW MATERIAL OF DECISIONS

The project folder in front of you represents information, both existing and possible. Information is the raw material of decision making; it is what helps you reduce uncertainty. The nature of information is one of my favorite subjects, so much so that I wrote a book on it called *Managing Information Overload* (AMACOM, 1996). For now, just remember that information is knowledge in any form. And sadly, you can't know it all. Give up that fantasy right now. But what you can do at "lunch" is organize what you do know.

Is your folder empty? If so, don't despair. The following exercises will help you pull information out of your brain that you didn't even know you had. You know a lot; you just haven't taken the time to pull it all together. Even more exciting, 30 minutes from now you'll have a much better sense of what you don't know. And you can then decide what's worth finding out.

A SERIES OF SORTS

The rest of this chapter represents a series of sorts you can do that will help you organize your thinking so that you know what to do next. You may even learn enough to predict what probably will happen and prepare for it. Your goal is to find patterns of reality and bring order to those swirling thoughts that keep you awake at 3 a.m.

Read through this list and pick out three sorts to do. Of course you can do more or less than that number. The main thing is that you don't need to do them all. And if this list inspires you to do some different sorts of your own, great!

Most sorts have three possibilities. The easiest way to do them is to take three sheets of scrap paper and write down one possibility across the top of each sheet. Call that your sort sheet. Then put the three sheets on the table in front of you. As you review what is in the folder, move it to the appropriate sort pile. As thoughts come to you, jot them on the sort sheets. My examples are short; you might have pages and pages. For whatever sorts you select, make two passes. First, sort what, if anything, is already in your folder. Next, go back and *think* about what you can add. Write that down too.

One final caveat: Things probably won't fit neatly into categories. So what? Does your day ever go exactly according to plan? That's why your pencil has an eraser. Just put your information somewhere and then come back and refine it later as the pattern begins to pop out more clearly. Also, set aside the time management rule of "handle a piece of paper once." When you are thinking, you may have to handle information many times till you understand what it is telling you. This is part of the complex game of life, and it's fun once you regard information as the pieces of a puzzle.

Sort I: What you know/don't know/suspect

Sort II: Frequency of occurrence: daily/weekly/monthly

Sort III: Time frame: past/present/future

Sort IV: Costs: past/present/future

Sort V: What works/half works/doesn't work

Sort VI: Big picture/today's problem/small detail

Sort VII: Like/neutral/don't like

Sort VIII: Rate of change: fast/slow/stable

Sort IX: Who is involved

Sort X: The fishbone: symptom/cause/effect

Sort I: What You Know/Don't know/Suspect

This sort is the most basic and is always a good one to do, so let this be your first pass. Once you get what is in your brain on paper, you may be surprised at what you know or don't know!

An unexamined fantasy exists that you should base your decision on "facts." The trouble is that facts are few and far between.

The purest definition of a fact is something that can be verified by your five senses: "I saw you there" or "I heard you say that." The reality is that facts constitute a small amount of your information. Instead, you are working with summaries, opinions, conversations, and computer reports with mistakes in them. Give up the belief that you can base a decision only on facts. Instead, sort your information into what you know, what you don't know, and what you suspect.

For example, Jason is a new supervisor with an employee named Karen who is often late, and he thinks he should talk to her. His information spread might look something like this:

What I Know	What I Don't Know	What I Suspect
Karen is late to work.	How many days last month?	She has day care problems.
This makes me mad.	Is she aware of how I feel?	I need to level with her.

Observation: I know Karen is late, but I don't know the frequency. Perhaps I am overreacting. I need to pull the time cards and see exactly how often she was late so that I can be more precise when I talk to her. Or I need to observe her behavior over the next 30 days so that I can talk to her about her attendance record.

As you sort your information, you can further refine your grid:

	What I Know	What I Don't Know	What I Suspect
Key info	Karen is late.	How often?	Day care problems.
Noteworthy	I feel angry.	How does she feel?	I'm overreacting.
Trivial	She has a long drive.	Does she carpool?	Where she lives is none of my business.

The trivial row is a great place to write down your indignation and then let it go. Such unprofessional outbursts probably won't strengthen your case, and writing them down makes its easier to keep things in perspective.

Jennifer remembers the time she wanted to hire a new marketing manager. She had worked with a really sharp guy who had been one of her suppliers for three years, and he had always had good ideas about how to sell their product. When she heard he was looking for a change, she quickly hired him. It was a disaster. She immediately realized that he had great concepts, but when it came to putting them into practice, he couldn't do it. After a three-month trial that was hard on both of them, he moved on.

In talking to me later, Jennifer realized that the information she had was not enough. She knew the guy was good at his current job. She knew he had ideas. What she didn't know and hadn't found out was whether he had the ability to implement his ideas. Upon reflection, she told me: "I wish I had given him a test during the interview, for example, to draft a press release. His lack of skill would have been immediately obvious, and I would have decided not to hire him." I assured her that she had made a reasonable decision with what she knew at the time. Things might have worked out. She comforted herself with the thought that she had learned from the experience. As a more experienced interviewer, the next time she would prepare work-related tests and quizzes that she could use to have candidates demonstrate skills.

Key question: How can you prove what you know to someone else? Can you back up your knowledge with reports, budget figures, articles, policy manuals, or copies of the law? Perhaps your next step is to be certain you can convince others of what you "know."

Tip

If you are a confident person, you may know less than you think you do. If you lack faith in your own abilities, you may know more than you think you do. Tending too far in either direction can hinder your ability to make a good decision. Putting your thoughts in writing will help you steer a middle course.

Sort II: Frequency of Occurrence

Do you have a problem worth solving? One of the easiest ways to determine that is to do a sort based on frequency of occurrence. How often does your situation really come up? Doing this sort will definitely help separate the trivial from the significant and the exception from the rule. Here is one way to label your sort sheet:

Daily	**Weekly**	**Monthly**
Break time abused by everyone	Karen late	Don and Brian late

If you prefer, another way to sort is:

Often	**Seldom**	**Never**

Then make notes under each section.

Karim was in charge of customer service for his small computer company, and he was pleased with the way the phone was ringing off the hook. His crew was busy! In a staff meeting, he reported that his technicians were overloaded; they needed to hire someone else right away so that customers would not be kept waiting.

One reason this company was prospering was that the team members were good thinkers. When a coworker asked what the precise nature of the calls was and the frequency of occurrence, Karim didn't get defensive. Instead, he said, "Good question. I'll report back next month." He returned to his team with steno pads and placed one beside each phone. Every person who took a customer call was requested for the next 30 days to write down the nature of the problem.

Karim was able to abandon the survey after 10 days because the reason for the calls was quickly obvious. Production had recently changed the way the monitor cables hooked up, but the owner's manual didn't reflect the change yet. At the next staff meeting, Karim proudly reported that the company didn't have a customer service problem. Instead it had a documentation problem. A team was quickly put together to update the manuals. Not only did the company save the expense of hiring a new employee, the real problem was solved.

Sort III: Time Frame: Past/Present/Future

If you are stressed out, one the of the best sorts you can do is to take apart your situation, breaking it down by what did happen, what is happening, and what might happen. Note the difference in these three conditions. The past is over; you can learn from it. The present is in progress; you may be able to implement changes right now. The future hasn't happened yet; you have time to prepare a response. Take your three sort sheets and label them as follows:

What Did Happen	What Is Happening	What Might Happen
Karen was late a lot.	She's doing better.	Boss will be impressed that I resolved the problem.

Are you worrying about the past, present, or future? Are all your entries in one column? If this is the case, you probably are out of perspective. Some people beat themselves up over the past; others obsess about the future. Seek balance.

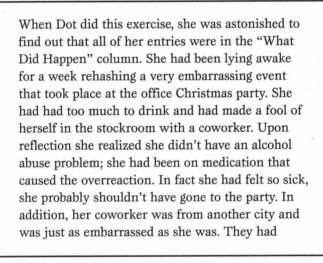

When Dot did this exercise, she was astonished to find out that all of her entries were in the "What Did Happen" column. She had been lying awake for a week rehashing a very embarrassing event that took place at the office Christmas party. She had had too much to drink and had made a fool of herself in the stockroom with a coworker. Upon reflection she realized she didn't have an alcohol abuse problem; she had been on medication that caused the overreaction. In fact she had felt so sick, she probably shouldn't have gone to the party. In addition, her coworker was from another city and was just as embarrassed as she was. They had

(continued)

already agreed to drop the subject. She concluded that there was nothing to do but forgive herself, consider the subject closed, and get on with the future. She patted herself on the shoulder, tore up and ceremonially discarded her sort sheets, and went back to work.

Sort IV: Costs: Past/Present/Future

Most difficult decisions involve money. Just what is this mess costing you, anyway? Here's how to find out. If your situation has already happened, take three sheets and use them to think about what money has already been spent, what the outflow is now, and what this situation could cost in the future. If you are thinking about a future expenditure, you might want to think about what failure to make the changes you are considering would cost. Remember to make these sheets work for you. Be prepared to have to go back and acquire information. This exercise will help you figure out what you are missing. Look at the following example.

Costs	Past	Present	Future
Known	$1,000/month	$1,350/month	Not available

You can further refine your grid by adding a second row separating known costs from estimated.

Estimated	Not available	$1,000/month	$1,500 (per quote)

Be aware that any entries in the "Estimated" row are far less certain than those in the "Known" row. Budgets aren't called dream sheets for nothing. Look for relationships between the "Known" and "Estimated" columns. Are they changing at the same rate? If possible, go back to old estimates and see how accurate they were.

Edd and Gail were considering selling their house and moving into a condo. Their kids were in college, and both had demanding jobs. Yard work had ceased to be fun. They took their checkbook register and totaled what they had spent on their house over the last year. Once they did that, they realized that even though their condo mortgage payment would be $100 per month higher, their total costs of housing would be far less because they no longer would have a yard or routine exterior maintenance expenses. They bought the condo.

Tip

Pretend you are in a staff meeting presenting your proposal or defending your position. What could you bring with you or make copies of to support your recommendations? Annual reports? Final budget figures? Income statements? Tax returns?

Sort V: What Works/Half Works/Doesn't Work

Here is a great sort that can help you pinpoint what the nature of your problem is. Your thinking will get clearer once you write down exactly where your concerns are centered. Note how the following example is labeled and completed.

What Works	What Sort of Works	What Doesn't Work
1 and 2 assembly drawings	assembly drawing 3	drawings 4 and 5— a disaster!

Underneath the columns you can also list things by categories, including products, people, departments, computers, procedures, and whatever else you come up with. Then the next step is to figure out why it happened and what you can do about it.

After your sort, challenge yourself about *how* you know what works or what doesn't work. When you go back to your office, what can you do to confirm your assumptions?

Sort VI: Big Picture/Today's Problem/Small Detail

It's easy to let things get out of perspective, and this sort will help you focus your time and energy where it counts. Not only that, small details can be changed quickly but the big picture could take years to examine. Remember our earlier discussion about situations that are bigger than you. Placing your situation along the scale of magnitude will help you figure out the urgency of taking action and determine how complex your fix is going to be. Take your sort sheet and label it as follows. Notice the example of a product with declining sales, in this case a video game.

Big Picture	Today's Issues	Details
Market is saturated.	Should we buy new tools?	Should we replace the software engineer?
Internet is taking over	Should we pursue HDTV?	Are there many suppliers?

Concerns: Technology is changing, and I don't know what will be dominant in three years. How can we build a product that can be adapted to any of them?

As you do this type of spread, notice where you have questions and where you are reasonably certain of your statements.

> *Tip*
>
> *Match the level of information with the level of decision to be made. For example, don't generalize about the size of the market on the basis of declining sales in just one state. If you are buying a car, one friend's bad experience may not fairly reflect the reliability of the thousands of that car model that have been sold. You might want to go to* Consumer Reports *instead, for example.*

Sort VII: Like/Neutral/Don't Like

Decision making has an emotional aspect, and here is a way to get those pesky emotions on the table. This exercise is useful because you not only can examine how you feel about your situation in the cold light of day, but also you can think about how others will feel. Granted you can't know how they feel, but taking the time to think about it will give you a chance to anticipate objections and go back and overcome the concerns of anyone who might object to your plan. Take your sort sheet and head it as follows:

What I Like   Neutral   Don't Like

Then make your entries about anything and everything. If other people are involved in your decision, do a second pass. Let's say you are thinking about where to go on vacation.

	What I Like	Neutral	Don't Like
Me:	Beach, golf	Where we go	Doing nothing
Gaye:	Beach	When we go	Long car trip
Brooke:	Malls	Beach okay	No other teens nearby
Brit:	Malls, movies	Open	Stuck with parents
Ed:	Golf	Beach	No night life

It was time for Helen to buy a different car, and she really wanted a four-wheel-drive vehicle. But money was tight, and she decided to think as clearly as she could. She suspected that for the big picture, insurance companies were going to raise rates because of all the damage a heavy car could cause. That meant her premium would go up. Today's issue was that she wanted such a car. When she asked herself why, she realized that (1) the car had high status and she wanted to impress her friends, and (2) it would be nice in the snow. She then asked herself if she was willing to pay an extra $4000 for a car to impress her friends. The answer was no. She also realized that when it snowed, she took the bus or stayed home. Finally, she realized she'd been influenced by the fact that she'd seen a cute car for sale in the showroom and had been waited on by a cute man. That certainly wasn't a good enough reason to spend the extra money. She decided that for this car she would lower her sights, but her goal was to save as much as she could from her upcoming raise so that next time she could get a fancy car.

On the basis of this review, the family picked a small-town motel on the beach with a nearby strip shopping mall that the kids could walk to. They figured Ed could take the car to drive to golf games, and the rest of them could be independent. A good time was had by all. Mom was especially happy because she didn't have to worry about her teens driving by themselves.

Another pass you could make would be to look at your list and see what you and others agree or disagree on. Then your effort can go toward building an agreement.

Sort VIII: Rate of Change: Fast/Slow/Stable

Another simple sort you can do is to review which parts of your situation are changing fast and which ones are stuck or going backward. This is especially useful when a reorganization or merger is planned. Not all parts of the company are affected at the same rate, and it helps to see what is stable and what isn't. That way you know where to place your attention and what can wait a bit. Review this technology marketing example.

Rate of change:	Fast	Slow	Stable
	Internet, telephone	Home computers	CD-ROMs

As a subset, you can refine the left-hand column by adding what is

Improving
Getting worse

If you have a situation that is getting worse fast, you probably want to get moving *now*.

Sort IX: Who Is Involved

Here is a really simple sort. All you have to do is make a list of who is involved. You'll be surprised how this list grows over time. It's easy to forget somebody on the first pass. Head your sheet as follows and follow the example described below.

Who Is Involved	Key People	Support People
	Vinai, Rosemary	Mark, Patt, Douangta

Tip

Nobody likes surprises. Involve the key people early. Not only do you want them on your side, they probably also have great ideas and could speed the project along. And if they have objections, ignoring them isn't going to make them go away. It's better to get it out on the table. And what about the support people? Would their input be valuable, contribute to team support, or be reassuring?

Mark reports, "My insights after doing this exercise were very different from what I anticipated. I had always regarded myself as a team player, contacting all involved and getting a consensus. But when I took a look at my list, I realized all those other names were a cop out. The decision was mine to make, and I had to do it. Involving all those other people was a waste of time. Not only that, I was really insulting them because their input didn't carry much weight and they knew it."

Sort X: The Fishbone: Symptom/Cause/Effect

This is the final sort and the most powerful one. When you are stuck, try this one. It helps you see a pattern and fix what is broken. The example below is my version of the fundamentals I learned many years ago as a management analyst with the federal government. It is often called the fishbone technique, because it looks just like a trout skeleton and because the situation hangs together the way a skeleton does. Experiment with this in a staff meeting; group input really strengthens the process. What you do is take your sheet of paper and make a drawing like the one below. Then insert your own symptoms, causes, and effects.

The fishbone: Symptoms   Causes   Effects

Symptoms are things that indicate that something is going on. They are flags. *Causes* are what make something happen. This is where you focus. *Effects* are results or outcomes. These are measures of success.

The Fishbone: Input - symptom - cause - effect

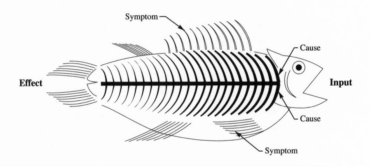

> **Tip**
>
> *Can you use a staff meeting to do an analysis of symptoms, cause and effect?*

It is very easy to confuse the three conditions, and if you do, you will fix the wrong problem. Remember our earlier example of the customer service department with too many phone calls? In that case, all the calls were symptoms. The cause was poor owner's manual documentation. The effect was overloaded employees. If the company had fixed the symptom of too many calls by adding more employees, the cause would have been untouched. The symptom might have disappeared, but at great expense and without creating happy customers.

SUMMARIZE WHAT YOU KNOW

There you have it; ten simple sorts to help you bring order to your chaotic thoughts. Now go to your folder and take your brain dump and start sorting. You may not get this done in one sitting. That's okay. Take it as far as you can and keep mulling it over. Don't be discouraged if your thoughts don't fit neatly. Just take those pieces of paper and place them where they make the most sense. Learn what you can. The real purpose of these exercises is to help you figure out what you know and what you still need to find out. Have you done that? If so, good job!

Restate your situation using more precise language. Use the sort sheets as headings for your statements. For example, I know that _____. I don't know whether _____. Or perhaps I suspect but need to find out if _____. Now compare that to the jumbled

After organizing a major report on the history of her company, Brit realized she had to protect more than the floppy disks of her writings. She immediately took all her chapter folders, which included photos, interview notes, and the names of all her contacts, and stored them in a fireproof filing cabinet. Those scraps and idea fragments may look messy, but they have been processed through the most powerful computer she possesses: her brain. She's taking care of them.

What do you need to put in a safe place?

notes in your brain dump. Are you impressed with how much clearer your thinking is? You should be. Congratulate yourself on the progress you are making.

It's almost time to get back to work. First, lean back and ask yourself what you have learned. What sort of sequences do you notice? Do you see trends? Can you identify what is causing your situation? Make notes on what you observe. Create a to-do list for information you still need to gather. Shrug your shoulders and let go of what you realistically can't find out.

CAPTURE FLEETING THOUGHTS

Even though your mind is now clear, you will still get ideas and have thoughts about all your situations. When such a thought comes into your mind, capture it by writing it down as soon as you have it. Your thoughts are the money your mind produces. Collect your thoughts as you would dollars, for they are the raw materials you will use to make your decisions. Don't worry about whether your thoughts are good ones. The process of evaluation will come later. For now, capture them. Your ideas are fleeting and will quickly be pushed out of memory by a new idea or distraction. Put your notes into the appropriate files.

Keep your thoughts in a safe place. Thoughts are valuable. If your folder is getting thick with lots of valuable information that has not yet been processed and is not available anywhere else, consider storing it in a fireproof file cabinet. Computer printouts can be recreated easily from disks. Your thoughts can't. Respect them.

Tip

Grab a scrap—a scrap of paper, that is—every time you feel an idea coming on. The way to do that is to have a pile of recycled scrap paper and a pencil everywhere. Attach the pencil to a chain if it is likely to disappear. (A very successful writer I know chains a pencil to herself. It looks weird, but she captures lots of good ideas!)

Locations include

Beside your bed

Beside every telephone

Beside every sink, toilet, and shower

In all the cars

In your purse and briefcase

On every conference table.

Add any other good places you can think of. Remember, the key is to jot down an idea the minute it comes to you. Doing so ensures that you won't lose it and frees your mind to concentrate on other things. In addition to paper, feel free to use tape recorders, voice mail messages, electronic notepads, and any other system that appeals to you.

> **Remember**
>
> Information is the raw material of every decision. Take the time to examine systematically what you know and learn what you can from it. The payoff will be enormous in terms of perspective on what has happened so far, insights into the cause of your dilemma, and clues about what to do next. Start off by mulling over what you notice, not judging it. That way you won't make up your mind or close off other options too soon.

MOVING FORWARD

Do you now know enough to make a decision? If so, do it. If not, you've learned a lot from the past. Now it's time to step into the future. Schedule another "lunch with Lynn," turn to Chapter 8, and prepare to do just that.

8 S: STEP INTO THE FUTURE

T hink about your situation as it exists today. Ask yourself the following questions:

Where do I want to be a year from now?

What does "success" mean to me?

How will I get there?

What will I do if things don't go as I planned?

As a thinker, you are going to ask yourself these questions. Your answers will provide direction and take you closer to resolution. The beauty of thinking is that you can learn from the past to savor today while preparing for the future. And you can do all your thinking at "lunch." What a banquet life is.

FROM TODAY TO TOMORROW

As you step into the future and picture your dilemma resolved, imagine the relief you will experience. Isn't it a wonderful feeling? The guilt of procrastination is gone, and your thinking effort has paid off. You know that you have done the best you can. Take a deep breath and burn that sense of satisfaction into your brain. It is entirely possible that hard times lay ahead; use the anticipation of those feelings of relief and satisfaction to keep yourself strong and determined.

The future cannot be predicted with absolute certainty, but by applying your thinking skills, you can often anticipate how things will turn out. If you like the outcome of your probable scenarios, great. Good times lie ahead. If you don't like what you suspect might happen, you still have time to plan some different strategies. All this is possible because you haven't done anything yet except invest time and brainpower. No money has been spent, and no people are involved. Think how much effort you will save because of what you don't have to redo!

Your goals for today's "lunch" are to

Picture success so you know where you want to go

Create options that might become a things-to-do list

Prepare timelines and see what is possible

Anticipate trouble and prepare for it

See if an obvious solution or plan of action jumps out at you.

Take a minute and let go of anything else that is distracting you. If necessary, clear your brain by making notes and reminders on a piece of paper and putting it aside. For the next 30 to 60 minutes you are going to concentrate on one thing: the project at hand. Also examine your attitude. Your job for today is to mull things over and examine possibilities. Don't despair; the time to judge will come—just not till Chapter 10.

One more piece of good news: Chapter 7 on examining what you know and this chapter on stepping into the future take the most intellectual work. After that, things will be easier. So keep going; the hard part is nearly done!

Terry was a new supervisor, and her consultants were terrific. All were highly educated, very professional, and supportive of her efforts. Even the man she had beaten out for the job told her he was learning a lot. Life was good. The only fly in the ointment was her trainee. Marsh had a great attitude and was very articulate. However, as Terry began to go over his draft reports in detail, she realized he didn't say very much. It was as if he took a list of long words and strung them together. At first glance it was impressive, but when she tried to use those words to figure out what to do, she went, "Huh? This doesn't make any sense."

Terry very much believed in coaching and devoted many hours to working with Marsh. She went out in the field to interview clients with him, helped him outline his draft reports, and gave him direction as many different ways as she could. But his work didn't improve. Terry began to lay awake at 3 a. m. wondering what was wrong with her ability as a supervisor. She even called Marsh's alma mater to confirm that he had been awarded a master's degree; he had. That made her feel even worse. He was a smart guy; she must be doing something wrong.

Finally, after six months, on June 10 at 4:10 a.m., Terry had a revelation: What if it's him, not me? she wondered. Maybe he's the one in the wrong job. At that moment Terry's determination began to build. Terry remembers the day vividly because on that day she began to document Marsh's performance. After 30 days Terry could clearly see that Marsh was unable to operate independently, a skill

(continued on next page)

required of a field consultant. Terry liked Marsh and wanted to keep him; then she pictured her life two years later with him still on the team. The image staggered her. She was redoing all his work; the thought of doing that for two more years was unacceptable. In addition, her clients were becoming increasingly sophisticated. One had actually asked her the other day if he was being billed for Marsh's time.

Terry finally had a serious talk with Marsh. She explained her concern that he was in the wrong job. After a 30-day period with no improvement, she told him that she would not recommend him for promotion to the next step in his series. He could stay where he was, as a trainee. Soon afterward, the pressure got to Marsh and he found another job in the organization.

Terry told me that she decided not to fire Marsh because he was honest and hardworking. Luckily, her company was big enough to absorb him somewhere else. She reports that he "fell off the fast track" but was a steady worker in his less responsible (and less lucrative) position. "It was picturing the future that gave me the strength to take action," she said.

THE WAVES OF RESOLUTION

Resolving your dilemma probably will take some time. Picture the resolution of your situations as the pattern of a wave with a building crest and an ebbing flow. A situation typically evolves like the one in the figure that follows:

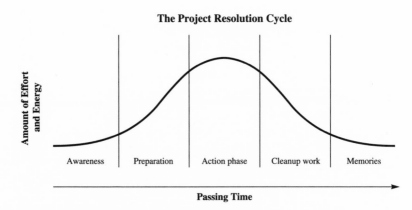

The phases of the wave are

Awareness: the first time you notice things are, are going to be, or should be different. The emotion is often concern or alertness.

Preparation: time spent getting organized, collecting information, and telling everybody what you are going to do. The emotion is often worry. (This is you today.)

Action: the period of time when your project is on the front burner, taking a lot of energy and effort. The emotion is often determination; you're just riding the wave.

Cleanup/Finish: the time of discipline that marks you as a winner. You document, file, and close out. The emotion is often boredom.

Memories: the phase of relish and great stories. Even the hard parts sound easy now. The emotion is often one of pride and satisfaction.

Note that the wave reflects time passing. Actual times to complete a project vary. Pick 90 days for a complete cycle if you don't have a better estimate. Situations don't resolve themselves neatly. You often start a project and then put it on hold as you wait for more information or a reply. What that means is that you are able to do more than one project at a time. In real life the process of resolution looks like the following picture:

**Waves of Resolution:
The project resolution cycle in real life**

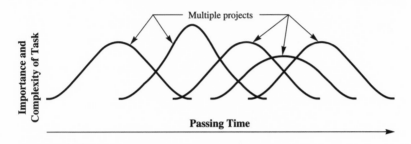

Ideally, one situation is cresting at a time. Certainly your stress level is reduced when situations are not peaking all at once. Conversely, you feel out of control when too much is going on. Obviously, you can't create a perfect system, but by becoming aware of the natural cycle of resolution and how long it takes, you can more realistically schedule your efforts and reduce the number of times when you feel out of control. Think of a person who drives you nuts because he or she rarely appears stressed. Do these people control their projects so that only one is cresting at a time? Just think how smug you'll feel when you too have time to "do lunch" at the last minute. In summary, give up any fantasy that complex issues are a quick fix. If they were, you smart person, you'd have had this project off your to-do list a long time ago.

PROJECTIONS AND POSSIBILITIES

In Chapter 7 you sorted out and organized what had happened before, including events, reports, requirements, and conversations. Now it's time for a mind shift to the future. To anticipate the future, you are facing a blank page of possibilities. How exciting.

The rest of this chapter will show to you how to use your imagination and brain to create projections and possibilities that can help resolve your situation. This is especially fun for all you "right-brain" creative types, for the sky is the limit. But guess what—it's fun for logical "left-brain" types too. You are a person with two sides to your brain, and today you will exercise both sides. If you don't consider yourself highly imaginative, don't panic. You've been able to understand everything so far, haven't you? This is your life, and you are perfectly able to create the future you want.

The four projections you are going to do include

Projection I: Picture success, including what is ideal and acceptable.

Projection II: Imagine options, including practical and far out.

Projection III: Consider consequences, from today to tomorrow and back again.

Projection IV: Prepare worst-case scenarios: What can you live with?

Get out a pencil and a blank sheet of paper and prepare to move ahead. Picture yourself peeling an onion. Tell yourself that by asking yourself more and more questions, you are leading yourself deeper and deeper to the core of what needs to be done. Just as in peeling an onion, at first it's overwhelming because there are so many layers, some of which are dry and hard to get hold of. But a sweet (and possibly teary) center of satisfaction does exist. And with patience, clear thinking techniques, and determination you will find it.

Projection I: Picture Success

Projection I requires you to *picture success*. After all, how will you know you've arrived if you don't have a clear picture of where you want to go? You want to make success very vivid in your mind.

Success is a tricky word that is laden with unexamined assumptions. Stop yourself right now if you are imagining perfection, for that is very unlikely to happen. Instead, start creating a mind-set of success using words such as *acceptable, reasonable, satisfactory, good enough, finished* and *done*. You may be disappointed and wonder if you are thinking too small or limiting your options. Possibly you are. But your situation is complex, and by being realistic you are creating a very strong possibility that you will succeed. You also limit frustration and disappointment when it happens that you don't succeed. Success builds on success. For each new situation you face, you can challenge yourself to take a slightly higher step. That is the way to make big dreams come true.

To picture success, lean back in your chair and first visualize what is ideal. Then lean back again and imagine what is acceptable. It is very important that you write your thinking down. That way, when the time to judge your ideas comes, you'll have something to look at and refine.

Take your sheet of paper and create a success projection grid like this with four parts. Here is an example using a cash-flow projection. Do one for yourself, adding the comments that come to you.

Success Projection Sheet

Cash flow for XYZ project

Ideal:	$3500 left over; all projects profitable
Acceptable:	Break even; income equals expenses
Don't want:	Tapping into cash reserves
Unacceptable:	Bounced checks and deficits

Thoughts: I would like to do this project even though it is a little risky. This is our slow quarter, and realistically I'm going to be lucky to break even. I probably can postpone purchasing the new equipment and cut out overtime. And if we have to feed the new project one more month, I guess that's to be expected. Need to alert staff this is the last time, however!

The main thing is to make your success projection very vivid. Be able to picture it in your mind as clearly as if it were a done deal.

If after trying this exercise you find that you are unable to picture success clearly, you have two choices. You can put your project on hold while you research and refine your thinking, or you can choose consciously to go forward without a clear picture of what will happen. Either choice can be acceptable, and each has consequences. If you have a clear picture of where you want to go, picture yourself as a little bulldog, tenaciously going forward and pursuing your bone. Even if other opportunities present themselves, you are not easily dissuaded. If you are unclear about precisely what you want, picture yourself like my Dalmatian dog, not too picky and genuinely delighted with whatever food comes her way. One is active, and one is passive. Your life will include both roles; which one is appropriate now?

The Alzheimer's disease was getting worse. It was time for Julie to put her mother in a nursing home. The decision was agonizing, but her mother was unable to live alone safely any longer. Julie didn't know anything about nursing homes and felt overwhelmed. But she had to start somewhere. Before doing anything else, she decided to visualize success.

Julie sat herself down and pictured her mother three months later. Since her mother's walk was shaky, Julie pictured her in a pleasant, sunny room close to the elevator and not too far from the dining

(continued on next page)

room. The floors would be tile because her mother's feet dragged on carpeting. She pictured a pleasant, probably older (and cheaper) building without any fancy landscaping. She sniffed experimentally. There was no smell of urine, which was very important to Julie. She imagined herself making an unannounced visit and saw everyone well cared for and not sitting in soiled clothes.

With a sigh Julie accepted the fact that her mother was a grump and therefore probably wasn't going to like anything Julie suggested. She regretfully let go of any expectations of approval or appreciation. She also realized she had better consult with a lawyer regarding power of attorney, as her mother was rapidly becoming unable to care for her own money.

Julie took a sheet of paper, listed her requirements, got out the Yellow Pages, and began telephoning to request brochures. She knew she would soon be overwhelmed with unfamiliar language, Medicare regulations, and confusing choices. Maybe it wasn't fancy or medically sophisticated, but at least she had a vision of what would constitute acceptable care in her mind. Three months later, as she was driving to visit her mother, Julie realized she had made her vision of success come true.

Projection II: Imagine Options

Next you are going to expose yourself—to possibilities, that is. Projection II requires you to imagine options, including practical and far-out ones. Notice the word *imagine*. That word is key because you are going to think in an expanded mode. Options are specific things you can do that will move you toward your goal. They may or may not be practical.

Isn't *options* an impressive word? It sounds vague and important. Try it out; brag to your friends that you are "considering your options." Using that phrase makes you sound like a Hollywood producer, doesn't it? You may not be a Hollywood producer, but the phrase is a good one for you to use too. Considering your options is another way of saying that you are mulling things over. Use the phrase to buy time, sound intelligent, and, most important, remind yourself consciously to consider a wide range of choices.

What considering your options really means is deciding whom to call, how much money to spend, how much time to take, and whom to involve. Remember your school lessons on how to write a story: Answer the questions who, what, when, where, why, and how. Answering those questions now focuses your options.

For example, let's assume that your back hurts and you have resolved to quit denying your pain and get professional advice. You are considering whom to call. The options you create for yourself are important. Each phone call points you in a different direction.

Are you going to call a chiropractor, acupuncturist, massage therapist, Chinese herbalist, or doctor of medicine? If you opt for the doctor, will it be a family practitioner, orthopedist, or sports medicine expert? Project the consequences of your options into the future. A visit to an MD often involves powerful and expensive prescription drugs; that's what the *medicine* in MD stands for. A visit to an herbalist often involves weeds and seeds of uncertain origin and untested outcomes. Only you can decide what is right, but be aware that the option you choose will point you toward a certain course of treatment. Before calling anyone, look forward in time. What steps do you feel comfortable with? Then call the best fit. Even more important, don't call someone who is not on your wavelength. Set aside those practitioners as "unappealing options."

The secret to creating good options is first to think big and second not to narrow your choices too soon. Often an impractical idea can be refined. Remember, the word for the day is still mull. What are your possibilities?

The what ifs. I find the easiest way to create options is to picture yourself floating among the clouds and asking, "What if I _____." Just as in "Imagine Success" in Chapter 4, each cloud represents an option. As you float on a sunny day, let your mind drift, suspend judgment, and examine the picture of the clouds below. Feel free to add your own puffy possibilities. Jot down the answers to your questions as you go along so that your brain remains clear.

The "What Ifs—"

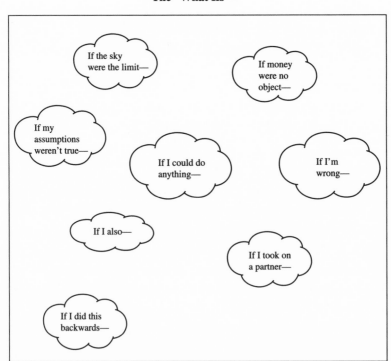

> ***Tip***
> *You have a lot more choices than you think you do. My personal observation after years of noticing how people make decisions is that people have far more choices than they realize. Most people don't lack choices. What they lack is imagination. They don't tap the power of their brains to come up with new ideas. Pretend you're a horse: Take off your blinders. Then get creative, just like Gillette did when he decided to make money on replacement razor blades, not on the razors themselves.*

Before you *do* anything, respect yourself enough to sit down and picture your goal. Then consciously think about what you could, might, and want to do to get there. What sorts of options do you have?

Jason had his own business making machine parts for the automotive industry, and he was tired of it. Life wasn't much fun anymore. He had worked so hard the last 15 years; was it ever going to end? When could he have some fun? Jason hadn't been self-employed these past years without becoming a good thinker, and so he scheduled a "lunch" to ask himself some hard questions. He was fortunate to have options. What were they?

First, Jason asked himself what his definition of success was. Many of his "successful" friends

(continued on next page)

played a lot of golf and really enjoyed it. Was that what he wanted? Should he join a country club? He shook his head as he realized that that lifestyle didn't appeal to him. Swatting a ball around a golf course didn't make his heart sing. He considered a red sports car but ruefully realized he didn't like exceeding the speed limit. What could he do?

He tried a different train of thought. What was he doing that he didn't like to do? That question provided him with insight. He realized that what he loved to do was tinker and experiment in his shop, and that he didn't do that anymore. Intellectually he knew that such work could be delegated to others and that working with his hands wasn't considered "status." But he had built his company from his skills working with lathes, mills, and drill presses, and he missed it! He didn't want fancy computer-controlled stuff either; he just wanted to bend, tweak, drill, and buff.

Jason had enough self-esteem and maturity to know that he didn't care what other people thought. He wanted to work with his hands and prototype again. Instead of plunking another $100,000 in the bank to go to his kids someday, Jason decided to spend $30,000 of his profits and buy himself some fancy tools. He figured that if his buddies could spend $30,000 a year on country club golf, he could spend that much on a machine shop. He returned from lunch a happy man.

Projection III: Consider Consequences

Now you are going to do some high-level thinking. Don't panic; it's not particularly difficult. But it's something successful people do all the time. Projection III requires you to consider the long-term consequences of your options. Have you ever been surprised by an outcome? Most people sure have. Some surprises are fun, but some aren't. If you spend the time to anticipate the long-term consequences of your actions, your surprises more often will be pleasant ones. What you want to do is use your mind to take you into the future and then back again.

Go forward. The first thing to do is create a forward timeline. Use the rule of three template to help you project what will happen if you do something, what will happen if you don't, and what will happen if you half do something by taking the middle ground. As your skills increase, you will become better able to project your life out over time. For example, as retirement looms, baby boomers are teaching themselves how to project income streams over time and determine the future value of money. It's better to start late than never, but as any financial planner will tell you, the earlier you have the skills to envision your future, the more choices you will have.

The rule of three. Use the rule of three to take you into the future. For example, ask yourself: If you do something, *then* what will happen in three days, *then* what will happen in three months, *then* what will happen in three years? You can use any timeline you want: one day/one month/one year works fine too. If you are thinking at the corporate level with a complex organization that is slow and expensive to change, your timeline might project out 20 years or more. For an individual, one to five years is a good place to start.

This exercise is called *If/then/then/then.* It builds on the last exercise, *What if* ? What if is a great way to create options; If/then/then/then is a great way to narrow them. Set time frames that make sense. Observe in the example that follows how Julie could use this exercise to narrow her choice of nursing homes.

If/ then / then / then

Choice A	Choice B	Choice C
If I pick nursing home A, the one near my work:	**If** I pick nursing home B, the one near my daughter's apartment:	**If** I pick nursing home C, not so convenient but with lifetime care:
Then in three days Mother will be easy to visit on my way home.	**Then** in three days, Mother will be handy for both my daughter and me.	**Then** in three days, I'll have a longer drive.
Then in three months Mother will still be handy.	**Then** in three months, Mother will be handy for us both.	**Then** in three months, I'll have a longer drive until I retire.
Then in three years I will be retired and this won't be so convenient.	**Then** in three years, my daughter will probably have moved but it works for me.	**Then** in three years, Mother won't need to move and I won't have to worry so much.

Julie concluded that it made sense for her to sacrifice short-term convenience for long-term security for her and her mother. She decided to find new dry cleaning, pharmacy, and other services along the route to her mother's. She also decided to start playing motivational tapes on her long drive both for self-improvement and to keep from getting depressed by her mother's criticisms and declining condition.

Back up. Another projection to help you narrow your options is what I call a reverse timeline. That means that instead of thinking from today out to tomorrow, you mentally put yourself into the future and work your way back. This is a great way to find out if

S: STEP INTO THE FUTURE

your time estimates are realistic before you set deadlines for yourself (and others).

To back up in time, complete the exercise *Before that/before that/before that*. What you want to do is picture your job done and then ask yourself what has to be done before that, before that, and before that. Confirm that backing into your timeline brings you reasonably close to the present. *Note:* If starting from your due date and working your tasks backward to today tells you that your project should have been started last month, you are doomed to failure. You need to refine your plans and expectations right now!

Abraham wanted to take the month of July off. He had earned two weeks of vacation time and wanted to ask his boss for two weeks off without pay. Before talking to his boss, Abe went out to lunch and worked through the following exercise.

Today's date: February 10
Goal: The month of July off

Before that, the inventory has to be complete by June 30.

Before that, the parts counting has to begin on June 1.

Before that, the damaged and surplus goods have to be balanced by May 1.

Before that, the inventory tags have to be balanced before April 1.

(continued on next page)

Abe also completed a reverse timeline that looked like this:

April	May	June 1	June 30
Balance inventory tags	Count damage and surplus	Count parts	Final numbers

Abe got the time off he wanted because he went to his boss with a reasonable request. He was able to show how he could get his regular work done and fit in the big project.

Projection IV: Prepare Worst-Case Scenarios

The final projection you want to do is the most emotionally difficult, but it is very important. You want to anticipate the awful things that could go wrong, the worst-case scenarios. This is the chance for all you worriers to shine. And for all you dreamers to force yourself to think outside the usual box. You don't have to change your personality, just expand its dimensions a bit.

The reason to picture your worst-case scenario(s) is because some consequences simply aren't acceptable. Sometimes, no matter what the odds of success, a 1 percent chance of failure means you don't try.

Complete this exercise by writing down your worst-case scenarios. After you write them down, ask yourself if you can live with your worst-case projection. Only you can answer this question. If your answer to yourself is no, simply discard the option and move on to something less appealing but less risky. All you need to do is take a sheet of paper and head it as in the example below of whether to apply for a new job.

The worst-case scenarios I can think of are _____

I am rejected and humiliated. (Short-term problem.)

My boss finds out. (That's easy: I'll tell her I'm looking to grow, which is true.)

I wasted time. (But an updated résumé is always useful.)

In this case none of the scenarios was too awful, so our thinker decided to go ahead and submit an application for the new job.

Tip
The assumption that "it'll probably work out" is faith abused. Faith in yourself and in the workings of the universe is the final sense of surrender that comes when you have done everything you can do. It is a calmness that you have earned. Faith that things probably will work out when you haven't taken responsibility for yourself is naive thinking and can lead to major life disappointments. Don't kid yourself that the worst-case scenario can't possibly happen to you.

Thamme was a human resource director. Her boss counted on her advice to keep him out of trouble and make him follow the letter of the law. She took her responsibility seriously. When he asked her a question, she would research company policy and write up a response. Then she would ask herself what other possible ways the memo could be interpreted. She would always show her memos to other people to see what they thought the policy meant. The employees were treated fairly, the company never got sued, and Thamme quickly was promoted to head of administration.

Sara was leading a snowshoe trip when she came to a long, steep hillside. At nine in the morning the snow was firm and stable, ideal conditions for kicking steps into the snow and putting in a route to the summit. But as Sara looked around, she realized she was on a south-facing slope and the sun was hot. In addition, the snow had just been dumped the previous day in a big storm and had not yet consolidated. The conditions for an afternoon avalanche were classic. Despite the complaints and disappointment of the less experienced members of the group, Sara aborted the trip. The consequences of an accident five miles from the closest road and 30 miles from the closest town were unacceptable.

ARE YOU DONE YET?

You've now reviewed the past and thought about your future. Maybe you're done thinking and ready to take action. Here are some questions to help you decide.

Do you now know what to do?

> If yes, go forth and do it. (Are you sure?)
> If no, keep thinking.

Can you draw any reasonable conclusions?

> If yes, what are they? List them.
> If no, who can help you?

Do you need to collect more information?

If yes, are you sure? Is it available? Is it worth the effort? Will getting more information reduce your uncertainty?

If no, will other people be convinced by what you can show them?

What do you *want* to do? Is it reasonable?

> *Remember*
> The best way to get the results you want is to envision them first and then work toward them. Good outcomes don't happen by magic. Instead, they are the culmination of many small steps along the way. By taking the time to mentally anticipate future consequences of your options before actually doing anything, you can more easily figure out what looks promising and what might not work so well. That way, when you do take action, your money and effort will yield far greater results. Use the If/then/then/then technique to help you project out in time. When you see ways to be even more effective or to prevent a problem before it happens, you'll be glad you did.

THE SUBTLE STUFF

Your thinking is nearly done. The final things to mull over before making a decision are subtle factors that may help or hinder you. Turn the page to get started.

9 0: OVERCOME THE SUBTLE FACTORS

BEYOND THE OBVIOUS

Y ou've reviewed the past and contemplated the future. A sense of certainty about what to do is building. But before you make up your mind, it's time to consider subtle factors that might bias your thinking and make you too optimistic or pessimistic. To help you, this chapter contains two due diligence checklists. *Due diligence* is an inexact legal term that means you've done your homework and exerted the effort and care a reasonable, prudent person would exert in similar circumstances. It's a fancy term for being thorough.

The exact amount of effort you exert depends on the importance of your decision. You probably don't need to do anything other than skim this chapter if your decision is a routine or trivial one. However, never forget about these checklists and come back to them whenever you plan a major undertaking. For example, if you are considering whether to spend more than $5,000, buy or sell a company, get married or divorced, have a child, move, or make any other major business or lifestyle decisions, take yourself to "lunch" and think through these intangible factors.

How do you know when you have finished your due diligence? When your shoulders sag, your mind ceases its whirling thoughts, and you say to yourself: "This is it. I've done all I can do with the resources I have available or that this decision warrants. Now it's time to decide, do something, and move on." That is what resolution feels like. Chapter 10 will give you guidance on actually making your decision. Your goal for "lunch" today is to complete your mental review of the subtle factors. By doing so, you will reap an enormous reward, gain confidence, and greatly reduce the chance of surprises.

This is the story of how two novice business owners (Nathan Roundy, my business partner-husband and I), successfully negotiated a six-figure software licensing agreement with a German company during our second year in business. The secret to our success was paying attention to the subtle factors involved.

The marine electronics industry is a small one, and so when Honeywell-Elac, a German company, wanted a jump start into the color fish finder business by buying existing technology, one of Nathan's former coworkers passed our name along. We were still operating out of the basement of our house when Herr Dr. Ludwig, the Ph.D. engineering director, and his staff came calling. They bumped their heads on our low ceiling but were unfailingly gracious as they poked the buttons on Fishscope I. Nathan's software was very innovative, and in 1982 we were "state of the art." We very quickly made a deal to ship them 10 units for testing and license the software if everything worked out.

The Germans were wonderful to us as we pinched every penny. We didn't have a telex (remember the days before faxes?) and so they suggested that we telephone our terse messages to a local Honeywell

(continued on next page)

subsidiary that would send them for us. Every time we went to dinner in Seattle they paid, which I have since learned is not the customary way to entertain international visitors. Finally we visited their impressive factory in Germany.

The final negotiations took place in the conference room in a historic building in Kiel. It was Nathan and I against 10 smart Germans. Things started off politely; but I knew we were holding our own when our hosts started speaking exasperated German to each other. They disappeared to caucus, and we sat there nervously reminding each other of the bottom line figure we would insist on. They returned and after much give-and-take reluctantly agreed to pay us our bottom-line figure. After the handshakes, with great ceremony they produced good French champagne for toasts all around.

The reason this negotiation worked was that Nathan and I had done our due diligence. I still have the steno pad we used to make the decision. There was a page for every possible issue we could imagine, including bottom lines and best-case–worst-case scenarios. We reviewed every iteration we could think of from market share per European country, to various pricing combinations, to tax consequences, to converting U.S. nuts and bolts to metric sizes. We walked into that meeting not knowing how things would come out but knowing we had prepared the best we could.

With hindsight I find our success impressive. A former government employee and a former marketing director held our own with a sophisticated, multinational company.

Good thinking paid off for us, and it can pay off for you too. The experience of negotiating that deal formed the heart of the checklists that follow. I hope you find them as useful as I do.

MORE THAN BUDGETS: WHY THINGS GO WRONG

Many people think the heart of decision making is figuring out what things cost and whether they can afford those things. That question is vitally important, and in fact this book presumes that you have fundamental budgeting and accounting skills. If you don't, take a class or go to the nearest bookstore *now*. Invest the time to get your personal finances on Quicken or a similar money management computer program; the benefits will be lifelong. But too many people stop thinking when the money question is addressed.

Have you ever made a proposal in a staff meeting that to you was perfectly documented and absolutely obvious? But instead of support for your good idea, a coworker looked at you, arms folded, and said, "But I don't want to do that." How do you respond? What pro forma budget computation, brilliant recommendation, or reams of computer printouts can you use to convince your colleagues? Logical proposals are good but not good enough. You operate in the real world of complicated human responses, emotional preferences, competing demands, and irrational forces. Success is more complex than just applying logic and reason. It's a combination of art and science, which is what makes it so interesting.

The purpose of the checklists in this chapter is to help you

Anticipate and prevent problems before they occur

Be fair and reasonable to yourself, your coworkers, and the company

Catch your own biases, because you do have them

Uncover different points of view

Be realistic but not shortsighted

Face unpleasant issues so that you don't kid yourself

DECISION MAKING IS A MESSY PROCESS

Decisions follow a series of mental steps that are invisible but very real. Sometimes you take all of them; sometimes you take short-cuts or skip steps. A big decision is a combination of many small ones. Your day is filled with decisions—most minor, some major—and cumulatively they form your life. You've heard this before, and you'll hear it again: You always have a choice, and that choice is to do something or do nothing. Therefore, decision making is unavoidable because doing nothing is one of the most powerful choices you can make.

Where did our society pick up the assumption that decision making should be a neat and tidy process? Sometimes it's hard to decide where to go to lunch, let alone which Friday night video to rent.

In decision making, analytic, left-brain processes are useful, but they are incomplete. For due diligence, what you want to consider is

Information that hasn't been considered anywhere else

The negative sides of positives and vice versa

Intended and unintended consequences

Costs that involve something other than dollars

DUE DILIGENCE CHECKLISTS

Review both of the following lists and note three or four items in each one that you want to think about more carefully. Treat this list as a springboard. Add your own items as thoughts come to you. Note that everything is in the form of a question. That's because only you can provide the answers. Get out your pencil and steno pad and start writing! You want to finish this review with a list of people to call and things to research or discuss.

Due Diligence Checklist I: Ten Subtle Factors Within Your Control

The subtle factors:

1: *Time.* Is this the "right" time?

2: *Resources.* Does this project represent the best use of your resources?

3: *Talent.* Do you have the talent to make this happen?

4: *Money.* Do you have enough money?

5: *Ethics.* Is this the right thing to do?

6: *Risks.* Do the risks exceed the rewards?

7: *Your preferences.* What do you want to do?

8: *Other people's preferences.* What do "they" want you to do?

9: *Emotions.* How do you feel about this project?

10: *Permanence.* How easily can your decision be changed?

Due Diligence Checklist II: Ten Subtle Factors Beyond Your Control

The subtle factors:

1: *Other people's perceptions.* What will others think?

2: *Mandates.* What do you have to do?

3: *Laws.* What are the legal requirements and implications?

4: *Formal politics.* What are the formal politics?

5: *Informal politics.* Where is the power?

6: *Industry trends.* What's going on around you?

7: *Economy.* How might the economy influence your odds of success?

8: *Mission and values.* What does the mission statement say?

9: *Other externals.* What other externals do you need to consider?

10: *Significant others.* What does your personal guru say?

Let us now analyze the first checklist.

1: Time.   You've looked at the calendar and prepared time estimates. Perhaps you have a preliminary schedule. Before committing to your project, put down your "day" planner and take one last look at your "life" planner, the big picture. Set aside what you "should" do. The question is, Is this the best time to resolve the issue? In other words, are you so frazzled that you can't think straight and one more task would put you over the edge?

Questions to ask yourself include: When does this decision have to be made? How long will it take to implement once you decide what to do? If you decide to do nothing, when will this window of opportunity come up again? Do you have other personal, professional, or psychological commitments that are demanding your time at the moment? Are you starting too early or too late? Is this the right season of the year? Is there any possibility that things might change in the predictable future?

For example, Terry was a consultant who had just earned his CMC (certified management consultant) accreditation. He could hardly wait to redo his brochures, proudly noting his hard-earned credential. He was at lunch doing a final proofread on his new design when he remembered a small article in that morning's newspaper about new areas codes coming to town. With regret and a sigh, Terry put his brochure project on hold because he didn't want to have to reprint yet again if his phone number changed.

2: Resources.   Resources include everything it will take to complete the project. You've already reviewed your needs for people, money, and time. Now lean back and reflect on what else you need. Take out your checkbook register or chart of accounts and note what you have written checks for in the past year. Add expense lines for any new items that should be included in the budget projections. Poor planners can go broke or lose everything by failing to do their homework. Put your thinking cap on!

Questions to ask yourself include: Have you considered what machines, equipment, and supplies you will need? What, if anything, is going to be hard to get? Are you depending on any sole source suppliers? Are your travel estimates realistic? Any chance of overtime requirements? What holidays may slow you down? What other costs are involved? Is there any group whose clout could take precedence over your promised resources? Do any items require a lot of maintenance? Can you order spare parts ahead? Do you need any written confirmations or approved purchase orders?

3: Talent. Perhaps you have assembled a team to help you with this project, or perhaps you are going to do it all by yourself. Either way, look beyond the official job descriptions of the people involved. Ask yourself if you and your team are any good at this sort of work. If not, what can you do to strengthen your talent pool? Otherwise, not only will your project not go smoothly, the end results may be unsatisfactory. For example, I learned the hard way that not every accountant knows how to adjust physical inventory valuations. On paper and over the phone, the CPAs looked and sounded good; in practice, they were not experienced. I was the one who suffered. Lack of talent is also a good excuse to get out of lots of chores; for example, it's much easier to avoid being drafted for yard work if you never learn how to operate or rethread that weed whacker!

Questions to ask yourself include: Are you or those who will be working with you competent to undertake this project? Do you have or can you get the human resources to make your project run smoothly? Is advance training required? Are you likely to experience staff turnover? Have you done this before? Do you or your coworkers have a flair for this type of work? Are you eager to learn something new and prepared to be frustrated during the learning process? Can you sign a contract, provide incentives, or get some sort of guarantees that key people will stay until the project is finished? Can someone else do this job better than you? Can you partner with them?

4: Money. The subtle analysis of money has two parts: Do you have enough money to complete the project, and does this project represent the best use of your money? Things rarely cost less than you estimate; don't create stress for yourself by getting in over your head with too much debt. Also, examine your values carefully to make sure that this expenditure of hard-earned cash is being spent on what is important to you and/or the success of your organization. Your challenge is to separate your self-esteem from money. You are not your money.

Questions to ask yourself include: Can you *really* afford this project? Do you have enough money to cover cost overruns and other unforeseen expenses? Is spending this money going to make you more money (an investment), or will the money be gone forever (an expense)? How many hours do you have to work to pay for this project (the cost of the project divided by your hourly wage)? Is it worth it? Are you spending this money for ego satisfaction or because you are unhappy, are seeking revenge, or are stressed out? Is this nice to have or necessary? Is this project worth a loan and the interest expenses involved?

> *Tip*
>
> *Call anything whose value decreases the minute you acquire it an expense. To build wealth (the freedom not to have to work), keep expenses to a minimum.*

5. Ethics. Examine your value system. Confirm that what you are planning to do is going to make the world a better place. If you aren't that noble, at least make sure you are doing no harm. If your task is difficult, prepare to build your character by persevering through tough times. It's worth it, for doing so will give you inner strength your entire life. Also, if your stomach hurts or you are having trouble sleeping soundly, examine your conscience. It may be trying to tell you something.

> **Tip**
>
> *Give up any expectations that you will be rewarded for doing the right thing. Sometimes you just have to be strong, do what you have to do, and seek support from a few special friends.*

Questions to ask yourself include: Who should you tell or not tell about this project? Are you creating any sort of hazard for employees or customers? How long will or should this product last? What is the environmental impact of your project? Is your packaging recyclable? Does your conscience hurt? Do you feel guilty? For those who won't agree with you, can you make a credible argument for your choice? What would a jury think? Could this send you to jail? Is your judgment call as reasonable as someone else's? Are you being shortsighted?

6: Risks. Chapter 4 in Part I of this book covered the concept of risk thoroughly. Please reread that material if you are not yet comfortable with the risks involved in your project. In addition to emotional risk, many projects present some sort of liability issue. You may want to bring your insurance policies with you to "lunch." There is no way to avoid risk. But careful thinking can help you come up with a plan to reduce your risk and tip the risk-reward ratio in your favor. In other words, it's far cheaper to call your attorney and insurance agent sooner rather than later.

Questions to ask yourself include: Have you listed and evaluated the risks? Do you have sufficient insurance? Will it cover what you are undertaking? How do you know? Have you read the policy to be sure? Have you requested a written ruling from your insurance agent? Can you get a rider? Are your subcontractors insured? Do you have certificates of insurance to that effect? Have you requested the litigation history of your partners? Do you have a large net worth that will be put at risk? If you get sued, what could you lose? Could your wages be garnished? Could you be considered criminally negligent? Do you still want to proceed?

7: Your preferences. Nowhere on a balance sheet or pro forma income statement is the question of what you *want* to do covered, but this question is vitally important. Typically, the higher up you are on the experience and income scale, the more choices you have. But even if you are considering your first job, your preferences must be considered. Contentment comes when you are clear about what you want and don't want and can meet your own needs. That usually happens at age 45 and up, so don't be discouraged if it hasn't happened yet. With maturity things fall into perspective.

Some people use the word *intuition* to describe a deeply felt sense of what to do. In my opinion, intuition is an integration of experience, unconscious reasoning, and complex combinations of insights that the western mind doesn't fully understand. Combining intuition with careful thought may help you make a good decision. Note, however, that bringing up your intuition in a staff meeting may not impress the boss. Don't use intuition as an excuse to be mentally lazy or fail to face reality; that's a recipe for disaster.

Acknowledge your preferences. For example, if you hate to travel, don't accept a job as a field sales representative. Try for inside sales instead. Conversely, if you are restless by nature and love to travel, think carefully before pursuing a profession, such as medicine, where people come to you. Even if you are stuck now, make choices that will open future doors and move you in the direction you want to go.

Questions to ask yourself include: What do you want? Is it reasonable? Are you embarrassed to state what you want? Does saying it make you defensive because it's not politically correct? Are you rising above your own biases by using neutral language to describe your preferences (e.g., "the supervisor," not "the jerk")? If you can't get what you want now, what steps can you take to increase your chances of getting it in the future? Do you need to reinvent yourself totally? Are your motives pure, or are you out to get someone? Do you need to see a therapist to figure out what you want? If you have no power to get what you want, can you let go of your disappointment and get on with your life?

8: Other people's preferences. Unless you are a recluse in a cabin, other people's preferences will affect what you do. In general, the bigger your company is, the bigger your family is, and the more dependent your customers are on you, the more impact your decisions will have on others. The converse of that, of course, is that the bigger your company, family, or customer base is, the more support you have. Thus, your choice is not between right and wrong; it's between balancing what you want and what others have a reasonable right to expect. As George Orwell said, "Some pigs are more equal than others."

Questions to ask yourself include: What do others want you to do? Are their expectations reasonable? Will your family support your choice? How about your coworkers, boss, support staff, and peers? What can you do to convince others of the merit of your choice? Will you succeed if you ignore them? Do you always "win," or is this truly your turn to prevail at last? Can you describe precisely the objections others have? Can you understand their point of view? Do you have the strength of mind to ignore pressure? If the others drop you from their circle, can you still function? Will acting on your decision force you to grow? Are you in a rut? Do you need to make new friends? Is it time to move out or to move on?

9: Emotions. First, accept that it is okay to have emotions; they are what make you human. What you want to do is accept your emotions, see if they are helping or hurting you, and find ways to rise above them if necessary. Remember, emotions are dangerous at the extremes. Fear is at one end of the continuum, and fear can be paralyzing. Euphoria is at the other extreme—the failure to acknowledge any possibility of failure, risk, or negative outcome. Do an attitude check. If you describe yourself as afraid to progress or absolutely certain things will work out okay, go on alert status. You may not be thinking clearly.

Confidence and quiet acceptance are the emotions of a wise thinker. When you feel those emotions, you are in the power zone. You sense that whatever the outcome, you can cope with it. Name your feeling. Is it one that makes you shrug and say, "That's okay"? If so, great. If not, you may be stuck until you change your mind—literally.

If you have reason to believe that your emotional responses are more extreme than those of other people, consider therapy with a mental health professional. It will be the best money you ever spent on yourself. Now may be the time to release the pain you are still carrying from childhood, a failed marriage, or another unhappy life experience. Emotions are a powerful part of your personal package; you want them working for you and your success. You want to be your own best resource, not your own worst enemy.

Tip

When you are indecisive because of emotional paralysis, ask yourself whether you are responding to feelings about yourself, about the issues or situation itself, or about other people. Being specific helps you break the logjam. For example, if you realize you are mad at the computer, you might as well get over it because the computer doesn't care. If you are angry at a coworker, perhaps you need to clear the air. If you are mad at yourself, maybe it's time for forgiveness.

Questions to ask yourself include: Are you sad because your choice will close off options and possibilities? Are you happy that your decision will bring closure? Can you name your emotion? Can you figure out how this emotion is influencing your behavior? How can you overcome the power of this emotion? Are you kidding yourself? Can you think of a friend or coworker who could provide perspective? Are you hungry? Tired? Getting over the flu or jet lag? Worried about something? Is this a bad time to decide anything?

10: Permanence. I believe life is full of second chances, as this nation's divorce and bankruptcy rates tell us. There are some exceptions; for example, the decision to have children is one of the most permanent decisions you can make. You are a parent, in spirit if not in shared housing, forever. That decision should be made very carefully. Certain results of your decisions are permanent, as a paraplegic victim of a drunken driving accident can tell you. But setting the exceptions aside, what you want to do is ask yourself how hard a poor decision would be to change and what it would take to regroup if that became necessary.

Questions to ask yourself include: How easily can your decision be changed? How much time would be lost if you had to start over? Is this a matter of taste? Personal preference? Life or death? Will you be able to salvage some, any, or many of your efforts if the project is abandoned? What time frame is involved—are you talking weeks or years of effort? Do you have a backup plan? Are you closing a door to the past or opening a door to the future? Is it time to move on?

Let us now analyze the factors that you cannot control.

1: Other people's perceptions. Perceptions are different from preferences. Earlier in this chapter you factored in preferences: what other people want you to do. Now shift time frames. Picture the deed done; ask yourself how you will appear to others. That is perception. In other words, when you think of people you respect, will they be impressed or unimpressed with you and your decision? You are always molding your future personal and professional reputation. If your decision improves your reputation, you will create future opportunities and open new doors for yourself. Whether you call it "selling out" or "being practical," creating positive perceptions makes people want to be associated with you. Often, making a few changes and minor accommodations is all that is needed.

Questions to ask yourself include: What will others think? Who will have an opinion? Do you care what they will think? Will implementing this decision enhance or harm your reputation? Is there anyone who will use your decision as an excuse to "get you"? Will this decision increase your number of supporters or foes? Even if people don't agree, will they admire what you have done? Will your friends stay your friends? In reality, will most people care? Are you setting yourself up for criticism by telling too many people what you plan to do? Is this a situation where you can't please anyone?

2: Mandates.   A mandate is a call to action, and it may be obvious or subtle. An obvious mandate is the need to upgrade a product line because of a competitor's new model. A more subtle mandate is the need to appear politically correct even if deep in your heart you'd prefer a return to the good old days. Look around you. What mandates do you see?

For example, if you are still recruiting for a "secretary" instead of an "administrative assistant," some talented people will not care to work for you because they will see your company as old-fashioned. People define themselves differently today whether you like it or not. For most companies, the need to adjust staffing strategies to reflect the changing workplace is a mandate in these days of labor shortages. Of course, a fancy title still doesn't take the place of a raise.

Questions to ask yourself include: What mandates do you have? Is your organization privately owned? What do the owners want? Is your organization public? What do the stakeholders and/or shareholders want? Will your corporate culture support your decision? Are your competitors doing it, whatever "it" is?

How long have they been doing it? How long can you put off doing it? Is the situation in flux? Will a standard evolve if you wait? Does it make sense to change your strategic plan? Upgrade, drop, or add a product line?

3: Laws.   In our society, laws usually exist because most people support them. For that reason, laws are one of the most difficult things for an individual to get modified or changed. In most cases you're better off finding out the requirements and complying with them.

For example, by the time a helpful (nosy) neighbor turned us in to the city for operating illegally out of our basement, we had nine employees. There was no question we were violating the zoning laws. Instead of doing battle with the city inspector, I said to him, "You're catching me by surprise. [true] I'm going to have to find a place to rent and move the company. How much time can you give me?" His reply was, "Because you're being so accommodating, I will give you the maximum extension of 90 days—instead of the usual 60—before we have to shut you down." You can guess what my next project folder became: "Move the Company." Realistically, doing so was the only option.

Questions to ask yourself include: What are the legal implications of your decisions at the federal, state, county, and city levels? Do you have or can you get the required permits, registrations, and certificates? If the government is not now involved in your decision, is it likely to become involved? Is there a risk that your project could be shut down and all your effort be lost? Do you know what taxes you have to pay? Do you need to see an accountant or attorney? Do you need to visit personally a government office? Have you started a file to keep vital records that you might need to produce some day? If you choose to ignore the laws, are the consequences serious? Will you get a warning? A fine? Jail time? Are you so indignant about all the forms you have to fill out that you want to run for political office?

4: Formal politics. While it may not be fashionable to admit it, chains of command mean that other people and departments have the power to help or hinder your project. Even for a one-person office, the bank and IRS still have to be accommodated. If you make sure to follow the proper procedures, usually your approval times will be shorter and your chances of success greater. If you work for a large organization, use the structure to your benefit. Tap the resources and talent that are available. Get your smart peers on your side. Great opportunities await if you involve people up front and generously share the credit.

Questions to ask yourself include: Does an organization chart exist? Have you reviewed it to see who might be affected by your project? Have you contacted the involved people? What approvals are needed? Do you need to check with human resources, an in-house counsel, purchasing, or accounting? Who will object to your plan? What can you do to accommodate their concerns? Do you need to schedule a planning lunch to sell your project? Who owes you a favor? Can that person intervene in your behalf? Have you listed the benefits to the various players? What smart person can you take to lunch to help you strategize for success?

5: Informal politics. Whether you are part of a large or a small organization, informal politics exist. Your challenge is to concentrate on increasing support from your peers. Peer relationships are the most complex because the balance of power is so fragile. You and your counterparts are equal but also are friendly competitors. Often the resource pool is limited, and so, for example, if you get the money or staff you need, someone else will come up short. The shift in focus toward teamwork and productivity improvement has greatly lessened the energy required to navigate the sea of informal politics, but crossing the wrong person can still be time-consuming.

Questions to ask yourself include: Who are your peers? Will they support or object to your proposal? Are you assuming what your coworkers will think, or have you asked them? What concessions can you offer if asked? Who do you need to call ahead of time to brief or ask for support? Who is "out to get you"? Can you mend fences now? Are there some people you should not call so that you can plead ignorance? Do you need to get down on your knees and beg and grovel and promise some people you'll help them next time?

6: Industry trends. Things change. By reflecting on the trends in your industry *before* you start spending money and effort, you'll save yourself the grief of being out of touch and obsolete. Good ways to find out what is going on in the bigger world include joining a trade association, reading professional journals, and attending trade shows and conferences. If you are now doing that, you are most likely current on industry trends. However, if the budget, time, or personal preference do not permit such "luxuries," be aware the times may be changing without your knowledge. For example, Marvin works in the timber industry and stays current on what "tree du jour" has an endangered species perched in it. Drew's laboratory used to market asbestos testing, but one day she realized that most asbestos would soon be removed or contained. She immediately redirected her efforts to focus on molds, spores, and mildews.

Questions to ask yourself include: What trends could affect your project? Will an emerging trend help or hurt your position? Are you playing catch-up or innovating? Do you need to delay your project till you see what shakes out? How can you get ahead of the trend and be perceived as an industry leader? Can you write an article to establish your expertise? Can you contact someone who has written articles for current information? Have you researched the Internet? Is one of your parts likely to become obsolete or hard to get? Do new parts, equipment, or computers that you'll be using have the bugs out of them yet? Do you want to quit while you're ahead?

7: Economy. The global economy is here, which means that just about everyone needs to look up occasionally and notice the really big picture. Things such as the North American Free Trade Agreement, the European Union, the emergence of the single

European currency, and the Asian shake-ups have affected even the smallest operation. Business opportunities can open up and disappear overnight. Even irrevocable letters of credit can be revoked if an economy gets fragile; trust me, I know. By noticing the world's changes as they happen, you can position yourself to take advantage of new opportunities or change direction before a distant event negatively affects you.

Questions to ask yourself include: How might the global economy influence your project? Do you tune in to the radio or television news or read a newspaper enough to stay current on industry changes? Do you need to accommodate different international standards? Do you need to go metric? Is your Standard Industrial Code changing? Is what you are importing or exporting hazardous, perishable, or fragile? Do you need to translate any of your materials into another language? Does international business appeal to you? Can you cope with jet lag and phone calls at weird hours?

8: Mission and values. Most businesses today have mission and value statements, and some of them even go beyond platitudes to provide useful direction. Even for yourself, you have a mission statement and values, though you may not have articulated them or written them down. Goal setting, values, and mission statements are beyond the scope of this book, but the exercise is well worth doing if it is new to you. For example, if you want to start a $1 million business, don't become partners with someone who wants to start a $100 million business, or, worse yet, a $100 billion business. Frustrations will abound because you're coming from different places, both of which are legitimate but incompatible.

Questions to ask yourself include: Have your examined your personal or professional mission statement recently? Are your goals written down? Do they give you guidance in this decision? Does what you are considering feel right or consistent? Would you tell your mother what you're planning? If you look five years ahead, is this decision taking you where you want to go? If things go badly, will the harm be irreparable?

9: Other externals. This item gives you a chance to add anything else that comes to mind. Whatever you think of, go ahead and jot it down. As the old saw goes, there is no such thing as stupid questions. They are far easier to fix than stupid mistakes.

One intangible that hasn't fit anywhere else is what effect your decision will have on your company's goodwill. Goodwill is the name given to the steady building of a company's value and worth in customers' eyes. Goodwill is not given a dollar value until a company is sold. Then the more goodwill the company has acquired, the more the brand name is worth and the more someone is willing to pay for the business. The equivalent at a personal level would be your reputation.

Questions to ask yourself include: What other subtle external factors can you think of to consider? Will your decision enhance your personal or professional goodwill? If you drop dead, would you like this decision to be mentioned in your obituary? Is your decision so trivial in the grand scheme of things that it's time to quit thinking and get moving?

10: Significant others. Who do you care about, and what special person cares a lot about you? In other words, why don't you call your grandmother or the equivalent and ask her advice? She probably has your best interest at heart and the fewest hidden agendas of anyone else you might consult.

Once you have used all these checklists, feel free now to consult taro cards, astrologers, the voices in your head, and any personal gurus you value. Perhaps these ethereal voices will provide one last perspective. Or maybe they'll help you tune in to your gut. Decision making is a messy process, and who am I to say what will work for you?

SNIFFING THINGS OUT

To finish your due diligence, take a deep breath and reflect on what you have learned. Pretend you are a bloodhound on to a faint scent. Sniff deeply and learn everything you can. Howl if you want to, but don't let go of that nagging thought until you have it in perspective. Study your notes. Are you now clear about what you are going to do? Have you learned something new that will take you in a different direction? Have your efforts reinforced what you already know? If so, great. You are ready to make your final decision. Are your concerns growing? Then maybe you need more time to ponder. What steps can you take to overcome your concerns?

> *Remember*
>
> Being a good decision maker means looking beyond what is immediately obvious. Written materials such as budget figures and reports are essential but not complete. Use the checklists in this chapter to help you consider the intangible factors that can contribute to success or failure. Being attuned to the "subtle stuff" is the mark of an expert decision maker. Your awareness will increase rapidly once you train yourself to look beyond the obvious and notice what is going on behind the scenes and on the sidelines.

Congratulations on considering the subtle factors. This careful thinking has greatly increased the odds that what you want to have happen in fact will happen. Whatever you now decide, you're going to do just fine because very little will catch you by surprise. Chapter 10 will show you how to pull all your careful thinking together and, one way or another, do something.

10 L: LEAP, LURCH, OR LAUNCH INTO ACTION

t's time to *do something*. You are now ready to make a decision, take action, and for better or worse let the consequences of your choice unfold. Note the change to a passive mind-set in the last part of that sentence. Once you've done your best, you have to let go and see what happens. Things probably will work out just as you anticipate. If they don't, interesting times lie ahead!

The good news is that if you have followed the steps outlined in the RESOLVE It! system, you have greatly increased the odds that your outcome will be just what you hoped. Your chances of success are high. You and your brain are a powerful team. Congratulations for all your hard work; now it's payoff time.

A "GOOD" DECISION

Have you noticed how this book has not focused on concepts such as winning, losing, beating someone, coming out on top, and getting the best deal? That's because those are value judgments some people apply to outcomes. Win-lose thinking reflects the traditional sports metaphor in which there can only be one winner and everyone else loses. Not only is such thinking old-fashioned, it's not true. Everyone can win. One reason I like mountain climbing so much is that every member of the team can reach the summit. Some are a bit slower to get there, but the view from the top is the same whether you arrive at noon, 1:30 p.m., or the next day. What a marvelously inclusive metaphor for today's diverse society. Forget about beating someone; just concentrate on reaching your peak.

If what you want to do is "win," that's easy to achieve. All you have to do is never take a chance. You'll succeed 100 percent of the time, but what a tragedy. You are condemning yourself to a narrow world in which you do the same thing over and over. You deserve more than that. You deserve excitement, exhilaration, enthusiasm, disappointment, disasters (they will make great stories someday), and joy. Reserve your pity for those who don't try, for their lack of confidence in their ability to cope and their desperate need to control their small worlds are condemning them to a lifetime of less. Vow to live your life large.

What is a good decision? To me, a good decision is one with few surprises, one in which your outcome is what you hoped it would be. That way risk is put into perspective. For example, if you apply for an opportunity along with several other talented people, of course you stand a chance of not getting selected. So what? If you don't apply, you know what your chances will be: zero, of course. If you give it your best shot, the odds in your favor certainly increase.

The reality is you will not always succeed and things don't always work out as you hope. When that happens, Chapter 12 shows you how to recover from disappointing decisions. But for now, let optimism reign.

THE APPROACHES: LEAP, LURCH, OR LAUNCH INTO ACTION

Here are three ways to approach your decision. Mix and match these styles in accordance with your mood and what your situation warrants. Have fun with it.

- *Leap.* Sometimes it makes sense just to leap into things. Especially if your decision is routine, minor, or trivial, make a decision and get on with it. Picture yourself in position for a standing broad jump. On your mark, ready, set, and go for it!

- *Lurch.* Other times your start is a bit rockier and tentative. Initially you start, stop, and perhaps lurch unsteadily. Picture yourself on water skis being dragged forward by the rope after a fall. Just hang on and keep moving forward. The important thing is not to lose momentum.

- *Launch.* The third approach is the strategic one in which you deliberately implement your quest for success. You have written plans, to-do lists, and a calendar. Stop right now and ask yourself: Are you launching a major effort in a minor situation? If so, does it make sense to redirect your efforts? Launching a quest for success is a great strategy if your situation warrants it. Remember, there is little reward for doing small things extremely well. Big rewards come to those who do big things. Seek excellence when possible and accept the fact that often "good enough" is, well, good enough.

No matter what style you use, the important thing is to *do something*. And this chapter will show you how.

THE ART OF JUDGMENT

At last the time has come to stop mulling things over and apply judgment. Judgment means you use your powerful brain to make preferences, to pick out what is the best fit for you. Questions to get you started include

Which is good/better/best?

What is acceptable/unacceptable?

What is appealing/unappealing?

What is suitable/unsuitable?

What will help/hurt?

What do I like/not like?

Note that applying judgment means you pick between at least two options. If you have only one option, then you are back to the key question of doing something or doing nothing. In fact, the toughest choices are when you have several acceptable or several unacceptable options. The rest of this chapter will help you wrestle with these types of choices.

Tip

Don't do things halfheartedly. Doing things halfway is a recipe for failure and often a form of passive/aggressive behavior in which you are preordaining your own disappointment. If you don't want to do something, face the truth and admit it to yourself. Say no if possible. If you are stuck, shrug and do your best anyway. Doing things halfway makes you appear weak, poorly organized, and wishy-washy.

THE STRATEGIES: ACT, REACT, NOT ACT

For every decision you face, you always have three choices. And those choices are to

Act: do something

React: passively wait for the situation to unfold and then respond

Not Act: do nothing

All these choices are appropriate sometimes. Your challenge is to match the appropriate strategy to your situation. Let's review them in reverse order.

Not Act

You can't do it all; therefore, you want to put your energy where it will do the most good. The decision not to act is a genuine choice. When you are sitting at lunch deciding what to do, before doing anything at all, ask yourself Lynn's key question: Do I need to do anything at all right now? Yes or no?

This question is one of the most powerful you can ask yourself. It is a fundamental principle of successful life management and one that few people follow consistently. Remember that doing nothing is a valid choice.

I must tell you that this idea came to me many many years ago while I was sitting through endless staff meetings. While I wiggled in my chair desperately wishing I were somewhere else, I was astonished to observe capable people spending enormous amounts of time discussing situations that they had no intention of addressing that day. All the talk was just that—talk. Nothing happened. The result was that meetings seemed interminable and real work was not getting done.

I vowed that whenever my time to manage came, my meetings would be different. And forgive me for bragging, but they are. At American Pioneer every time we start to drift away from the situation in focus, someone pops up with the reminder question: "Hey, wait. Do we need to do anything about that right now?" Often the answer is no, and we settle back down and refocus our efforts. Other times we look at each other with eyebrows rising and say, "Good point. How does it affect _____?" Are we perfect? Certainly not. Do we drift less than people who never ask that question? Absolutely.

If you will make the simple question, Do I need to do anything about this right now? second nature, an automatic part of your response system, your stress level will drop because your concentration is focused, the amount of available time will increase because you are not wasting minutes and hours discussing hypothetical situations, and real work will get done. Instead of talking

Caryn and Willem had the next phase of their life all planned out. They were each going to work five more years, saving every penny they could to build up a cash reserve, and then they were going to sail around the world. They figured that in two years they would buy their boat and live on it. That way they could fix it up and do local cruising while they improved their skills.

For the present, they planned to spend their weekends looking at used boats and doing a little dreaming. Two months later, while walking the docks, it happened: They found the perfect boat, and it had a for-sale sign on it. But it was too expensive. Six months later they were walking the docks again. And guess what? The boat's price had been cut 20 percent. The boat was exactly within their budget and just what they wanted.

They went out to dinner to talk things over. At first they were so excited about their good luck that exotic destinations such as Cabo, Tahiti, and the Canaries rolled around their tongues. Their checkbook was out. Then they caught themselves. Both of them had very demanding jobs. The reality was that if they purchased the boat right then, it would be an added stress, not something to enjoy. Plus they had not arranged moorage or sold the small cabin that would be part of the down payment. With reluctance they put the checkbook away. It was a great boat, but it wasn't the only boat in the world. They concluded that for them, the best thing for the next two years was to stick to their strategy and do nothing but work hard.

> Martine had just rented her old house as a duplex to two graduate students. Shortly after they moved into their respective units, she had a message on her voice mail to please call about the furnace settings. Martine was very conscientious and had just picked up her phone to respond when she slowly set it down again. When she asked herself if she had to do anything at all right then, she realized that probably the smartest thing was to give the guys a few days to work out a compromise on the temperature of the house. When she checked in a week later, she asked if there was anything the residents needed her to do. Both men said, "No, everything is fine." They had worked things out for themselves. For Martine, doing nothing was a good choice.

it, resolve it. Try this question out when you are by yourself at lunch, worrying in the middle of the night, or in a staff meeting. The results will astound you.

When is not to act a poor strategy? When doing so takes away a choice or a window of opportunity closes. Another self-test: Is it possible that you are procrastinating? In that case, reread Part I.

React

Passivity has its place. Sometimes the best thing to do is sit back and see what unfolds. Earlier in this book the rapidly changing nature of health care was mentioned as an example of a complex situation that no single individual can do much about. Sometimes you really do have to wait and see what happens and then make a decision.

Armand owned property on a busy street along
the waterfront, and he wanted to redesign his
parking lot. The docks were busy with both pleasure boats and fishing boats full of activity.
Delivery trucks and ice trucks were always coming and going. Old abandoned railroad tracks that
were nearly obliterated ran along the shoreline,
and one day Armand got a notice that the city has
holding public hearings on a request to turn the
railroad tracks into a bike path. Armand was
undecided. Bicyclists would be a nice addition to
the ambience, but the combination of heavy
trucks and hard-to-see bicyclists was a recipe for
accidents waiting to happen. Armand decided that
he didn't have strong feelings either way and
would wait and see what happened. Once a decision on the bike path was made, he would rethink
his ideas about a parking lot.

Interestingly, his neighbor, who ran a small delivery business involving lots of trucks, immediately
formed a task force to study the issue. The outcome
was important to her business, and she wanted to
provide input. Being passive was not a good strategy for her.

Two other ways to react are buying time and stalling. Buying
time means you negotiate with someone to delay a decision by
mutual consent. Stalling means you put off someone who really
would like you to move sooner. Both techniques can be appropriate.

Fritz, a staff director of a small professional association, was having a disagreement over the executive compensation policy with one of the board
members. The issue was scheduled for discussion
at the executive session that day, and just before
the meeting Fritz noticed that he had an urgent
phone message request to call that board member.
When asking himself the key question (Do I have
to do anything at all?), Fritz decided that his best
strategy was to ignore the phone request, to do
nothing. He suspected that nothing good would
come of a private conversation; he preferred to
have all the discussions be public and involve the
entire board. Fritz quietly crumpled up and discarded the phone message.

Act

Now we come to the option that will be developed in the rest of
this chapter. Do you choose to act, to take action, to make something happen, to just do it?

The first observation is that to act means you commit to getting something done; it doesn't mean you have to do it yourself. So
before you determinedly set forth on your quest, pause and ask
yourself if there is anyone else who should be involved either to
help you or to take care of the situation. Especially if you are a new
team leader or first-time supervisor, the temptation is strong to
"do it all yourself." Resist it. Other people have lots of talent. Tap
them and free yourself up for something else.

Also before you commit to action, ask yourself, Is this my decision to make? Similar to unfocused talk at staff meetings, trying to

make a decision that isn't yours to make is a waste of time. If this question makes you sheepishly admit that you are treading on other people's toes (and territory), either approach the key person and suggest a team approach or, as Ann Landers would say, "Mind your own business."

THE ROLE OF LUCK

Decision making is a messy process, and luck—like intuition—is a factor that doesn't fit neatly into the left-brain, analytic model preferred by business schools and traditional decision makers. I have no opinion on the existence of luck except to observe that it is a term often used by the less successful to describe the hard work and careful thinking of others. "She got lucky" usually means that she got what she worked for.

However, I do believe that the more you improve your thinking and decision-making skills, the luckier you'll be. My observation is that at least some of what we call luck stems from a quality of alertness. Many people hear the same casual remark in a conversation. Only a few pay enough attention to pick up on the opportunity that lurks in that casual remark. Fewer people still ever follow though. Those people are really lucky.

> *Tip*
> *"It'll probably work out" is a very dangerous*
> *assumption. True, it'll probably work out if the*
> *money in dispute is $5,000 and you have $100,000*
> *in the bank. It'll probably work out if you are hav-*
> *ing a squabble with your spouse and have been*
> *happily married for 15 years. But for just about*
> *everything else, the odds are a lot more likely to*
> *work out in your favor if you go to lunch and think*
> *about how to make things work out.*

DECISION STRATEGIES: GUIDELINES FOR THE UNCERTAIN

Complicated issues have lots of answers. Here are some techniques to help you narrow your choices and pick one. First, review your project file and list your options. Now read the list. Does one choice jump out as a winner? If so, great. Do that. If nothing pops up, try one of these techniques.

Technique I: Take the Easy Way Out

Is it possible you are making things too hard for yourself? Are you agonizing unnecessarily? Are you *procrastinating*? If so, return to Part I of this book. If not, use the following questions to help you pick the option that has the best chance of success. Go back to your notes on Chapter 8, step into the future, and firmly fix the ideal outcome in your mind. Then pick the option that

Fixes the cause, not the symptom

Is what you want to do

Is what others want you to do

Is the "right" thing to do

Meets the requirements

Follows existing policy

Is easy, cheap, and/or quick to implement

Comes up heads in a coin toss

Meets any other reasonable criteria you come up with

Are you surprised how simple these questions are? I hope so. Because you're right: You have known all along how to make decisions. All you have to do is be a bit more systematic and your success rate will soar.

> *Tip*
> *Do you have to justify your decision to others? If so, be sure to document your thinking and be prepared to explain your rationale.*

> **Tip**
> If all your options are equally appealing or unap-
> pealing, it probably doesn't matter which one you
> choose. Either choice will be good enough. It's just
> that different choices probably will take you down
> different paths. Remember to look forward in time
> and see if where you want to be in a year or two
> provides any guidance. If not, get out your coin and
> get on with your life.

> **Tip**
> Practice on small stuff. Remember that decision
> making is learned behavior that improves with
> practice and good technique. Practice your tech-
> niques the same way you practice tennis or jogging.
> First, just do it; second, try to do it better each
> time. Pick some small, nonessential decisions in
> your life to practice on for two months. Then go out
> and do big things.

Technique II: Rate Your Options

If one option does not immediately present itself as the best, you
want to rate your options. That means using a systematic method
to apply quantitative or qualitative values to your choices, totaling
the values, and doing what comes out with the highest rating.

Lest you become impressed with the implied science of those
multisyllable words, remember that you are the one deciding how
much weight to add to each of your choices. Decision making is a
messy process, and what you are really doing is organizing your
thinking, not applying a mathematical or statistical principle. Of
course, these grids and forms are very useful in convincing others

of the merits of your choice. Orderly thinking is far more convincing than no thinking at all.

> Ashley was an exceptionally gifted scholar who had her choice of top-flight graduate schools. Both business and law looked appealing. She couldn't decide. Finally, while looking forward in time, she realized that any of her choices would be satisfactory. There was no big downside risk to any of them; she just had to pick one. She was ready to flip a coin when she also realized that she wanted a life with some adventure. She then decided to specialize in international patent law, figuring she would work with growing businesses, travel a lot, and probably be able to live in many places.

Count your pluses and minuses. The first thing you can do is complete the grid below, noting the pluses and minuses of each of your options. Pluses and minuses are the same as pros and cons, the good points and bad points. Look at the following example.

Brett's situation: Should I buy a house now?

	Pluses (Pros)	**Minuses (Cons)**
If I do it:	No more rent; property inflating	High payments; maintenance expense
If I don't do it:	Keep cash cushion; stay mobile	Will cost more later

Thoughts: All my friends are talking about buying houses. I must be careful not to get sucked into their expectations. I'll take another look after I get my professional certification and a raise.

Count your pluses and minuses by numerical weights.
Now, if you want to, you can assign weights, which means you
give each pro and con a number from 1 to 10, depending on how
strongly you feel about it. The higher the number, the more value
you give. Pros get positive numbers, and cons get negative numbers. Notice that there is no rocket science involved. You just apply
your best judgment.

The totals point you in a direction because you do whatever
number comes out highest. For example, the house chart might
look like this:

Brett's situation: Should I buy a house now?

	Pluses (Pros)	Minuses (Cons)	Total
If I do it:	No more rent: + 10	High payments: – 10	
	Property inflating: + 2	Maintenance expense: – 3	– 1
If I don't	Keep cash cushion: + 5	Will cost more later: – 2	
do it:	Remain mobile: + 10		+ 13

Thoughts: Everyone else may be buying a house, but the reality is
that I expect to be transferred in a year or two, possibly to a small
town where real estate will be cheaper. My salary is going up,
and I am saving lots of money. I'll keep renting and help my
friends move on weekends. Buying a house right now is not right
for me.

Assess the benefits and risks.   Another way to make a decision is to pick the choice that involves the most benefit or the least
risk. Mark a "high" benefit when the rewards are high if you succeed and failure could result in little harm. You can write down the
benefits, put check marks in the boxes, or assign numerical probabilities on a scale of 1 to 10, with 10 being the most probable. The
main purpose of this exercise is to help you systematically summarize your thinking and get direction. Because you are anticipat-
ing your future, there can be no absolute answers. Be content with
directions, trends, and possibilities.

Benefits:	High	Medium	Low
Option A (describe)			
Option B (describe)			
Option C (describe)			

Complete the same exercise again using risks instead of benefits. A high risk means that the chance of failure is great or that failure could be serious. A low risk means that things probably will work out or that it doesn't much matter they don't. Either describe the risks for each option or assign numerical values.

Compare the benefit and risk charts. What do you notice? These exercises are good ones to complete over the course of time. Keep your worksheet on a desk or table. As thoughts come to you, continue to note them. Be sure to schedule a completion date, though. You don't want to revert to being a procrastinator!

Rank-order your preferences. Another thing you can do is describe each of your options on separate three-by-five cards. Then sit down at lunch and shuffle the cards, putting them in rank order with what you most want to do on top. Use the bottom of each card to note your reasoning. On the back of the cards note the counterarguments to the ranking. Finally, create a written one-page summary that is a form of commitment. Number one is what you are going to do! The rest of the numbers summarize your thinking about what you are not going to do and why.

GROUP DECISIONS

This is a book about individual decisions, not group decisions, but I do want to make a few points to help you put things in perspective.

Tap *Your* Group's Resources

First, realize that a group of fine minds is a tremendous resource for you. Even if you are a sole proprietor, you can create a group whose expertise and different perspectives can help you gain insight and make better decisions. Complete the following grid to help assemble your own group of resources. After preparing your intelligent questions, start calling, networking, and making lunch appointments. Remember, sharing wisdom is a two-way street. For every call you make, you are creating debts to repay. Be ready to defer your priorities and to help others when they tap you.

Group Resources

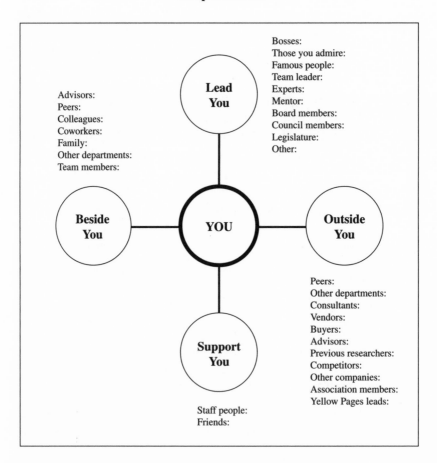

The Role of the Group in Decision Making

"No (wo)man is an island; no (wo)man stands alone." Let those eloquent, now politically correct, words of the poet John Donne remind you that most of your decisions involve others and are made in groups. Applying the synergy of many wonderful minds does many things, including uncovering new insights, creating consensus, providing the perspective of history, and detecting problems sooner. And of course if everyone truly feels part of the decision-making process, implementation goes far more smoothly and esprit de corps is enhanced.

However, groups are not a perfect vehicle for decision making. All the involvement and interaction take time, agreement may not be forthcoming, and the resultant compromise may not be the best solution. Another factor to consider is that everyone in the group may not be equally qualified to contribute, in which case people become timid or feel demoralized because they have nothing worthwhile to say. In addition, some people don't care what happens very much or even worse, may totally change the direction in which you had hoped to go. In short, groups have both risks and rewards.

The main thing to remember is that the strength of the group comes from the quality of the input of its members. The more able the thinkers, the more powerful the group. As the members of your group become better at resolving their own situations, the group probably will need to meet less often, such meetings (whether virtual, over e-mail, or in person) will be shorter and more productive, and the time spent on futile discussions will decrease. Think individually first and assemble into a group later.

Consensus as Fantasy

Please give up the fantasy right now that everyone in a group or team is going to agree on everything. In fact, sometimes it seems like no one can agree on anything. There are times when trying to create a consensus or even involving the group in decision making may be a poor strategy. For example, if time is critical, your expertise is greater, or your input is what counts, don't involve the group. Instead relish your (brief) role as king, queen, or dictator; *tell* the group members what to do; and get going.

CREATE AN ACTION PLAN

Take a deep breath and relax. You've done it. You've now considered all those confusing options and brought them into a semblance of order. You have no illusions that your thinking, or for that matter your decision is perfect. But you do feel confident that you have made the best decision you can with the time, money, and resources available. Good for you. You truly are a thinker. Congratulations.

But don't get smug. Now that you have made up your mind, you have to do something. It's time to translate those abstract possibilities in your mind into phone calls, purchase orders, assignments, meetings, letters, due dates, and all the other myriad activities that constitute an action plan.

Creating and implementing an action plan are not the focus of this book. Let me add a couple of suggestions, though.

Assign Specific Responsibility for Tasks to Someone

You want to make sure that your action plan assigns responsibility to a name, to a specific person. Responsibility may be assigned to you, to a coworker, to a subcontractor, or to a sales assistant in a retail store. It doesn't matter who is responsible. It does matter that someone is responsible. Just remember Murphy's law and have a name you can check with if (when) things go wrong. Put this in writing in your project file. Let the accountable person see you do it. Give him or her copies of anything in writing where appropriate. Don't be afraid to hold people, including yourself, accountable. It shows that you care.

Assign a Specific Due Date

At all costs you want to avoid idle talk and no action. You've worked too hard for that. The way to avoid inactivity is to assign a specific date on which the project will be started, reported on, or finished. It is essential that the report date be written down, at a minimum on your calendar, and that the accountable person knows you look at your calendar every day. Just like the elephant, you never forget. When you say, "Let's talk about your progress on June 10," you are on the phone that morning. Your word means something; you get results.

Keep a Running List of Details Still to Be Resolved

Your decision evolved over time; so will your plan. Every time you get a new thought, just add it to your to-call, to-write, or waiting-to-hear section. Don't let this evolutionary process throw you. It's called being flexible, and it's part of life.

Do You Need a Backup Plan?

Chapter 12 deals with what to do when things don't turn out as you anticipated. But this is a good spot to ask yourself—before changing the status quo—if you need to create a backup plan. Some plans are worth the effort; some are not. In general, if human life, major assets, or tremendous effort is involved, have plan B in mind, and possibly plan C.

TRUST YOUR JUDGMENT

You're ready to step out of your mind and into your future, to go from the abstract to the concrete. It's time to let go of your fear and live your life. Isn't this exciting? You have decided what to do, and you're doing it.

Trust your own judgment. Why not? Look how carefully you have weighed, measured, consulted, and debated. Your due diligence is done. Your chances of success are as good as anyone else's and far better than most people's, for you are a thinker.

Test your emotions. How do you feel? For some people, the narrowing of options and the making of a commitment represent a regretful moment. All the things that might have been have been narrowed to just one thing that will be. For other people, the narrowing of options and the commitment to action create a feeling of relief. Whatever emotion you are feeling, savor it and know that it is temporary. Tomorrow is going to bring new decisions to make and new emotions to feel.

Are you uncertain about how things will turn out? Have you had the guts to assume some risk? Remember that uncertainty is a temporary condition. One way or another, you'll learn your results. Meanwhile live in the present, watch your life unfold, and savor the satisfaction of seeing your plans turn out just as you anticipated or the surprise of the unanticipated.

DONE AT LAST

When are you done? When is the decision-making cycle complete? Consider yourself done when your project folder is tossed for recycling, filed, or put away until a future review date. You are done when there are no longer any action or cleanup items on your calendar. Truly being done probably will take longer than you anticipated because of the final cleanup, including thank-you letters and notes to the file. Allow time and respect the process of finishing things up and completing loose ends. Finishing what you start is what marks you as a professional and what makes people want to work with you. Don't forget the process of evaluating how you did, the subject of Chapter 11. Remember the sine wave on page 153. Your curve is flattening out; you're near the end of a cycle now.

Decision Record

For the record, here is my decision.   Date:

Present Situation:

Goal / Desired Result:

Decision / Actions:

    ☐ Do nothing

        ☐ Forget about it

        ☐ Get more information by _____

        ☐ Review again on _____

    ☐ Do something

        ☐ Plan A _____

        ☐ Plan B _____

        ☐ Plan C _____

Notes:

Next time I'll:

One symbolic thing you can do is create a decision record using the sample form on the previous page. Then stick it in your file. Some day you'll chance upon it, and reviewing the form will provide an opportunity for you to reflect on how your life has unfolded.

Be sure to note your major decision points on your calendar. All you have to write down is "Applied for XYZ team" or "Look at new space" to note when you are beginning. Then, when you are done, note on your calendar, "Joined XYZ team" or, sadly, "Didn't get on XYZ team." For the space note "signed new lease" or "renewed lease" to show closure. The point is that these very simple tricks can provide points of reflection and give you accurate estimates of how long things really take. It's part of the fun of decision making.

> *Remember*
> Until you do something or consciously decide not to do something, you are a talker, not a doer. Processing possibilities is fine but is not what gets your job done. Judicious action is the hallmark of a successful decision maker. You always have at least three choices: to act, not to act, and to react. Use all three approaches and use them consciously. Don't forget that every time you let something slide, you are making a very important choice, and that is to do nothing. Is that what you want?

HOW DID THINGS TURN OUT?

There's a final step people often forget: the opportunity to evaluate how things came out. For all you scorekeepers, turn to Chapter 11.

11 V: VIEW AND EVALUATE YOUR RESULTS

CONTINUOUS IMPROVEMENT

Continuous improvement means that your life is unfolding day by day and that you are a work in progress. Tomorrow you can be smarter. Tomorrow you can know more than you do today. The secret is to pay attention to what is going on and teach yourself how to do better the next time. Isn't that a comforting thought? While our society does not revere age the way some societies do, the fact remains that accumulated years of living can add up to wisdom. All you have to do is keep growing with the world as it changes, take reasonable risks, and learn from your mistakes. Then your eyes will sparkle and life will be filled with terrific people and interesting experiences.

One way to learn and grow is to assess realistically the results of your decision and determine what, if anything, you can do differently the next time. Most of your decisions will turn out well. In that case you want to determine what things you did right so that you can do more of them in the future. Conversely, when the results of a decision are disappointing, you want to figure out what, if anything, you can do differently the next time. Those lessons you can use to keep from repeating your mistakes. Therefore, whether or not your decision turned out the way you hoped, you have valuable lessons to teach yourself.

Chapter 12 will cover "bad" decisions and what to do about them. One secret to self-acceptance and self-forgiveness is to comfort yourself with the reality that (1) there were some things you didn't or couldn't know when you had to make your decision and (2) you can teach yourself to do better. By reflecting on what worked or didn't work, you can apply those lessons when "next time" comes.

This chapter shows you how to view your results realistically and then evaluate whether those results were satisfactory. Your goal is to apply those lessons so that you make better decisions in the future. Notice the two parts of this process. You first step back and objectively describe your outcome; you observe what happened as a neutral outsider might. Then you evaluate, that is, apply judgment, and congratulate yourself or lick your wounds.

TIME TO EVALUATE

When you get busy, it's easy to put off reflecting about what has gone well or not so well. That means you miss an opportunity to capitalize on your natural talents or perhaps keep on doing what you dislike or aren't very good at for far too long. The last thing Friday afternoon and the first thing Monday morning are natural times for evaluation as you organize the upcoming week. Try adding an extra 15 minutes to your planning and to-do list process; these few minutes spent will result in hours saved.

Evaluations take concentration but not necessarily a lot of elapsed time. Match the amount of effort you spend evaluating with the significance of the decision. Generally speaking, major decisions are worth major evaluation time and vice versa. An evaluation can be as short as 10 minutes or as long as months if your project is a major one involving longitudinal sampling of the results over time. If you don't know how much time to allow yourself, start with one hour.

You can do your evaluation formally or informally. If the decision is an important one, do a formal evaluation. That's an impressive term that means you schedule a "lunch" with yourself, gather your project folders, and give yourself some quiet time to think and make notes in a place where you won't be interrupted. If an informal evaluation is sufficient, take a few minutes while stuck in traffic or while waiting for your boss to become available to jot down a few notes to yourself and be done with it.

In either case, be sure to document your thinking with notes you can use to do better the next time. If you don't summarize your observations, you are performing an academic exercise, which is a fancy way of saying lots of talk (even if only to yourself) but no action. *The main reason to evaluate is to do better the next time.* You want to clear your mind of this decision so that you can concentrate on the next project, write your thoughts down, and file them where you will find them the next time you need them.

How long after implementing your decision should you do an evaluation? Do it as soon as you have perspective. That means you may be able to wrap things up the same afternoon, or it may be the next year. If you are so close to your decision that you are emotionally involved, your evaluation will be biased. In that case you are wasting your own time. Even though it's frustrating, you might as well wait until you are ready to learn.

> **Tip**
>
> *If a year has passed and you still can't be objective about what happened, consider going to a therapist for professional help. A year is long enough to work most things through and find closure. If after that time you still get emotional about the events, you're probably stuck and need extra help working through your version of posttraumatic stress syndrome.*

CHAPTER ELEVEN

EVALUATE WHAT'S IMPORTANT

By now you realize that not all decisions are worth major time and effort. Sometimes you just need to do something and get on with it. Similarly, not all decisions have to be evaluated. There are always exceptions, but here are some general tips to help you decide when a review is worthwhile.

Do *not* evaluate when:

- *The situation was a one-time event.* For example, if you know you will never again host a one-time special event, do your best and turn your energy to other things.
- *The event was a trivial one.* Remember the caveat not to do unimportant things well.
- *It's over.* Sometimes there is no second chance. You just have to shrug and move on.
- *Your results were good enough.* Perfection is an elusive ideal, and often "good enough" is!

Evaluate the results of your decisions when

- *You can teach yourself something.* Here is the best reason to view your results and evaluate them. Teaching yourself what you did right and what you did wrong is one of the best investments in yourself you will ever make. Note that you are not moaning and groaning; you are learning. There is a distinct difference.
- *The same situation or a similar one will recur.* This is continuous improvement at its best. If every time you do something it gets better; you are a success! For example, if your job involves hosting an annual conference, an evaluation and debriefing after the event definitely are called for. That way you will remember to do more of what works and less of what doesn't the next time around.

- *You are dissatisfied with the results.* Dissatisfaction is a major driver of change. Don't just worry in the middle of the night about what you did wrong or regret. Sit yourself down and see what you can learn.

- *Change is predictable.* If your results were satisfactory but your environment is changing, make some notes to yourself now so that you will be prepared the next time around. For example, let's say you got a one-time good price for something but your supplier has already advised you that next time the item will cost more. Capture any thoughts you have now about what you will do next time. That way you can avoid panic and budget crises. Don't plan to remember the price increase because that will tie up brain energy.

- *It's time for closure.* Sometimes the only way to let go is to give yourself a quiet "lunch" to review what happened, have a private little pity party, and forgive yourself and others if necessary. Then you are mentally ready to move on.

VIEW YOUR RESULTS

The first part of the evaluation process is simply to sit down and view, that is, note, what happened. To do that, get out your trusty yellow paper tablet and pencil and start writing. Use objective language and describe what happened. You will add judgment later. For now, use a time sequence, starting at the beginning, going on to the middle, and concluding with how things came out.

The use of objective language is essential because otherwise you risk being unable to assess what *really* happened. In other words, don't make up your mind too soon. For example, if you start off describing your results (and possibly yourself too) as a failure, you have already made up your mind before considering all the possibilities. Remember that a judge hears the evidence before rendering a verdict. Conversely, if you go into denial and tell yourself everything is okay when it isn't, you risk a serious credibility gap with the rest of your friends, teammates, and so forth. Have you ever heard someone referred to as a "dreamer"? That is another way of saying he or she is out of touch with reality.

Your description can range from a simple sentence to an elaborate report with an executive summary. Use your judgment to match the amount of effort with the importance of the event. If necessary put your notes onto the computer, into a fancy format, or in a momentous-looking tome. But remember, this event is over. Generally speaking you're better off getting this evaluation finished as quickly as possible so that you can move on to another interesting project that awaits you.

Tip

Vent wisely. Venting is the process of letting off emotional steam by using exaggerated language. It is a healthy outlet when done occasionally in a safe setting, such as off site with a trusted friend. In a staff meeting it is far more professional (and far safer) to use neutral language that objectively describes the situation.

For example, say, "The boat was tidy, but the seats had bird droppings on them and the bilge was emitting an unpleasant odor." That's far more professional than "That X % # left the boat a # % $ mess with bird # % $@ all over and the #$$ bilge stinking like ## % $. Those guys are pigs, and I bet they live in a sty." The reason is that "those guys" probably have long memories about your transgressions they would love to bring up. Alas, the ability to resolve it declines rapidly in proportion to the number of epithets hurled.

ASSESS YOUR RESULTS

Now that you have described your results using objective, professional language, you are ready to apply judgment, to assess your level of success. It's time for another key question, and that is: How did things turn out? Your response is one of two choices: okay or not okay.

Okay Results

If in your judgment the results were okay, good for you! It's time to congratulate yourself, and Chapter 12 will provide tips on how to do that. But don't jump for joy yet. Instead, finish your assessment. Sit down and bring to conscious awareness what you did that worked, any techniques that were unusually successful, people who were helpful, and pleasant surprises. Conversely, note what you might do differently next time.

Self-confidence is directly linked to the certainty that you *know* you did a good job, that your results were okay, satisfactory, or even excellent. Other people's praise is nice but you can fool them. You can't fool yourself. Tell yourself when you did well. Who else is going to do it for you?

Do you detect passion in my writing? I believe in self-reward very strongly and confess that I learned this lesson early. As a child in the fourth grade I had to cook dinner one night a week for my family and quickly became famous for bringing my offerings to the table and earnestly saying, "My, this is delicious, isn't it?" With hindsight, it was the beginning of true self-esteem. Of course, it also was a defense against my siblings gagging and choking on my scalloped potato and Spam casserole.

I believe that most people do not give themselves enough positive feedback about what has worked for them. Thus they miss the opportunity to build on their successes. You are a capable, thinking individual, and you are the one best able to provide yourself with useful information about how you did. Just take the time to

do it. Note that you are not providing yourself with empty platitudes or a trite "Attagirl" or "Attaboy." What you are doing is far
more powerful. You are taking your own behaviors and capabilities seriously and upgrading them just as you do with your computer.

Not Okay Results

If in your judgment things did not turn out okay, you have several
choices, and this chapter lists them in the section on replacements,
reworks, and apologies. For now, just be aware that sometimes
things will turn out okay and sometimes they won't. Life goes on,
and so will you.

Dangers of Denial

Accepting the fact that your results are disappointing (okay, admit
it: the whole thing was a total, unmitigated disaster) is adult
behavior. Disappointment happens to everyone and is the down-
side of risk. But you can cope, and Chapter 12 will give you ideas
on how to bounce back from bad decisions.

By far the greater problem is to kid yourself that things are
okay when they aren't. Then you risk failure at every level. First,
you miss the chance to truly resolve your situation. All denial
does is push the problem into the future. Wishful thinking
doesn't make things go away; it just narrows your options.
Second, you risk being perceived as unsuccessful by your peers.
Recovering from a poor decision is a sign of success. Denying
that a poor decision even happened is a sign of a person out of
touch with reality. And people out of touch with reality don't get
promoted but find that opportunities keep passing them by.
Finally, you miss the chance to grow and learn from your mistakes. In short, don't kid yourself. You certainly aren't kidding
anyone else.

WHAT HAPPENED AND WHY?

The primary purpose of your evaluation is to find out what happened and why. That way you can get to the root cause and truly resolve your situation once and for all.

One good way to do that is to use the fishbone technique that was discussed in Chapter 7 and is illustrated below.

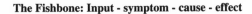

The Fishbone: Input - symptom - cause - effect

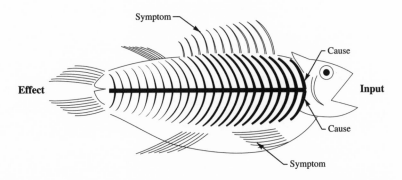

This time, however, your challenge is somewhat easier because you have the benefit of hindsight. You know how things turned out and have far more information about inputs, causes, and unexpected turns of events. The fishbone is a valuable technique to practice at every step of the decision-making process.

RATE YOURSELF: A SELF-ASSESSMENT QUIZ

Remember that for the purposes of this book, a good decision is one with few surprises. A bad decision is one in which you were caught unaware or for which you failed to prepare adequately. With that in mind, the self-assessment quiz that follows can help you summarize your thinking:

CHAPTER ELEVEN

Self-Assessment Quiz

Rate yourself from 1 to 10, with 10 being the most satisfactory.

Questions	Your self-rating
1. Did you meet your goals?	_____
2. Were you within time and money estimates?	_____
3. Were your results good?	_____
4. Were other people pleased?	_____
5. Did you break new ground and not repeat old mistakes?	_____
6. Do you want to do this again?	_____
7. Did you have fun?	_____
8. Did you develop and/or give back to others?	_____
9. Did you think for yourself?	_____
10. Did you make the best decision you could with the resources you had available at the time?	_____

Feel free to add notes to yourself at the bottom of the page. Make this an essay test if you wish. A key aspect of closure is to clear your mind. This is your chance do it.

Now tally up your score and save the test in your personal self-assessment folder. Give yourself this test over time. You'll know you're improving your decision-making skills as your self-assessment scores begin to climb. Congratulate yourself as you enter the 80 and 90 percent ranges. You have earned your thinking cap.

OTHER PEOPLE'S OPINIONS

Many times other people are involved in the evaluation process. This is certainly the case if you are involved in a team effort. If you provide a service or product, only the customer can determine

Karla was a real estate agent who had just moved to a different company, and she quickly realized her new office was a disaster. The computer system was antiquated, and the network was not well maintained. In addition, without a database of comparable sales to use in establishing house prices, she knew she could not remain competitive. She approached the office manager with her concerns and was dismayed to see him become defensive instead of open to suggestions.

She took herself to lunch to view and assess her situation. As she objectively described the nature of the office, she realized the situation was very complex and not easy to remedy. She concluded that it was time to cut her losses. She first telephoned a colleague who had always said, "Call me if ever you're looking for work." Alas, he had just filled an opening. Finally she decided to swallow her pride and call an old employer. Her heart quivered, and she dreaded making the call. But her old boss was delighted by the call and invited her in for an interview that day. She emerged with an offer of work and a better financial split than she had dared to hope for. (Turns out that after she left that office many years earlier, her boss finally realized what a good income producer she was. He was delighted to get her back.)

Although she figures that job shifting cost her a month of lost commissions she also knows that she will quickly regain her efficiency and lower her stress level in the better-managed office. Karla told me, "The only reason things turned out as well as

(continued on next page)

they did was that I faced the facts immediately. I'm rather embarrassed that I didn't research that office as well as I should have or could have. But at least I didn't let things get any further out of hand." Quickly and realistically evaluating her situation meant that Karla moved quickly to cut her losses and move on to a better job situation.

whether your offering is good enough. Use this exercise to help you put your feedback and that of others into a semblance of order.

As you talk to people and gather data, you can summarize information by using a grid like this one:

Results Summary

	Excellent	Good enough	Unsatisfactory
Your opinion:			
Others people's opinions (list names)			
Overall evaluation			
Comments and notes			

Again, the purpose of this book is not to provide a complete evaluation system for a complex project. The main purpose of this exercise is to separate your opinion from those of others. Then notice where they agree or disagree and determine which carries more weight. The thing to remember is that your opinion is separate from that of others and that your opinion counts too.

DATA COLLECTION AND INFORMATION INTERVIEWING

Often to evaluate properly, it is necessary to get feedback from other people. One of the best ways to get it is to interview them individually. Your goal for such interviews is to make sure you get solid information. You also want to be careful that you don't inadvertently cue people about what to say or subconsciously give them feedback that causes them to be less than honest. Use these techniques to improve your ability to ask good questions and gather reliable information from committee members, coworkers, and direct reports.

1. *Give the interview your ALLS:* **A**sk a question, **L**ean back, **L**isten, and **S**hut up. Resist the urge to put words in the interviewee's mouth. Instead, ask your question in the most neutral language possible, assume a pleasant expression, and then sit back and shut up for 10 seconds. If you have trouble doing this, count 1001, 1002, 1003, up to 1010. Wait for the interviewee to tell you what he or she is really thinking. Phrase the question the same way to each person you interview.

2. *Make use of the rule of three.* When can you be satisfied that you're getting reliable information? Try this guide: When three different people in three different departments have told you the same thing three different times, the chances are that you're on the right track.

3. *Zip your lip.* Don't gossip. People share information only with those they trust. A decision maker who violates confidences in the smallest way will end up making future decisions all alone, and his or her ability to manage will be curtailed severely. Pass on absolutely nothing. That includes smirking, shrugging, knowing winks, and other body language.

4. *Zip your briefcase.* Treat your notes as confidential. Keep them in a file folder labeled "Economic Projections for Malaysia" and take them home or lock them up at night. Remember, other people can uncode your scrawls, read upside down, and interpret or misinterpret your notes if they have the opportunity.

5. *Listen to weirdos.* Make a list of people who can provide different perspectives. Seek out people who don't look, smell, and think like you or each other. Consider seeking insights from bosses, peers, coworkers in other departments, support staff, and customers.

6. *Challenge everyone.* Most important, don't forget to question the boss. Do it politely but be definite and specific. Does he bluster and get defensive? Or does she smile wryly and say, "We're working on that." Challenge the big cheese and learn if you're dealing with an open and objective person. If you're the boss, have lunch with someone who will challenge *you.*

7. *Don't trust big talkers.* Look for discrepancies between responsibilities held and results claimed. Does it really make sense that this trainee was entrusted with approving final estimates, as she claims? Your antennae should go up when you hear such statements.

8. *Toss out a teaser.* Throw out a challenge question to see how the interviewee responds. Does he say "Yes, sir/ma'am" to every question? Does she have insightful opinions? Does he have any opinion at all on this or other issues?

9. *Smell trouble.* If your brain tells you one thing but your gut tells you that things don't add up, trust your gut and keep interviewing.

10. *Get permission to quote.* Even for favorable comments, confirm that each subject is willing to be quoted.

Moving comfortably in the messy world of missing, confusing, and unclear information is the mark of an expert decision maker. Remember, fact-based decision making is a fallacy! Say good-bye to that fantasy along with other favorite fairy tales. Good decision making comes from combining all those facts, opinions, estimates, summaries, and wild guesses that make up the realities of the workplace.

REPLACEMENTS, REWORKS, AND APOLOGIES

After evaluating the results, are you satisfied? Forget perfection. Instead ask: Is the outcome good enough? If the answer is yes, congratulations, you're done! If the answer is no, it's time to ask yourself the key question again: *Do I need to do anything at all right now?* Yes or no? Here are some questions to trigger your thinking and, if necessary, permit you to clear your conscience.

If you answer yes, you are dissatisfied with your outcome. Do you need to

Fix what's broken, again if necessary?

Replace what you never should have borrowed?

Apologize for the remark you wish you had never made?

Revise your estimates or recommendations?

Rework your offering, which deep in your heart you know isn't good enough?

Redo a report or letter?

Refund money that didn't provide good value?

Change a procedure to fix the root of a problem?

Announce a new policy to everyone?

Add your own fix here.

Do these questions look familiar? They are the essence of what good customer service is. When deep in your heart you know things aren't good enough, fix them.

Perhaps your answer to the key question is that although you are disappointed, the reality is that the results are good enough. You don't need to do anything at all except

Give it up

Let it go

Move on

Give it a rest

Cease

Stop

Write it off

Forgive yourself and stop the broken record player in your head

---

Tip

Don't let sunk costs sink you. In plain English, don't throw good money after bad. The money is spent, and you aren't going to get it back. Turn your efforts to the future and see what makes sense.

THE ROLE OF CHANGE

As you evaluate, look for the role of change in your situation. Change is important in decision making because it forces deci-

Ross had money and his brother had time, and so they decided to form a real estate partnership. They bought a small duplex to spruce up, and the project turned out well. Ross put up more money and they bought a bigger, six-unit building. It was a disaster. The units were not separately metered, and so the utility expenses skyrocketed. Plus the big plant in town had an unexpected layoff, and many of the renters lost their jobs and thus the ability to pay the rent on time. As cash flow got tight, Ross lent another $2,000, and then an additional $5,000 to meet the expenses. His brother asked for more.

Finally Ross sat down and assessed the situation. He sadly realized that pouring more money into the buildings probably would not save them. His initial down payment and the loans were a sunk cost, and in this case investing more money meant losing more money. He told his brother it was time to either sell the buildings or talk to the bank about their options. His days of investing more money had ended. Ross vowed that never again would he invest money without doing a careful analysis *before* writing the check and that once he owned something, he would evaluate it each quarter so that bad situations would be faced early on.

sions. As long as things remain the same, you don't have to do anything. You can maintain the status quo if you want to. But when things change, your options open up. You can merely note the change and do nothing, or you can choose to do something. And if you choose to do something, many possibilities exist.

Keep on the lookout for change; it signals opportunity. Order—the lack of change—is comforting because it reflects the past that you are used to. But change is exciting because it is bringing your future. You don't have to like change; you just have to notice that it is happening. If you deny what is going on, or can't face it, you lose valuable reaction time, time that others are using to good advantage. Besides, you can't stop change; you might as well make it work for you. Keep these thoughts in mind if you work in health care and other fields that are likely to be volatile for some time.

CLOSURE

Finally, not only your project but your evaluation is complete. Only a few small details are left to do now. The first is to make any notes for "next time" in the project folder. This is a very important step. Not only does it ensure your success in the next go-round, it also frees your mind from trying to remember things. The notes don't have to be fancy. Just take a sheet of paper, head it "Notes to the File," add today's date, and write away.

Question: Do you need to set up a system to monitor events on an ongoing basis? Some projects require this; some don't. Perhaps a notation in your calendar the first of each quarter to check things is sufficient. If you need an actual monitoring system, it's time to get books or take classes on project management. Don't reinvent your own wheel; good systems already exist—just not in this book.

Remember

Even though you have decided what to do and done it, don't consider your project finished until you reflect one last time on the results. Viewing and evaluating outcomes present tremendous opportunities to learn how to do better the next time, make any necessary corrections for things that didn't turn out as well as you'd hoped, and reward yourself for all the good decisions you made. Assessing results is a lot of fun and represents thinking at the highest level. You get to uncover the mystery of how and why things happened, notice the role of emotions, and experience the satisfaction of a job done and most often well done. Now take a deep breath, shake your shoulders, give yourself a break, and prepare for your next great adventure.

After finishing this evaluation process, either you're satisfied with how things turned out or you're not. In either case, turn the page for lessons on how to savor your success or lick your wounds.

12 E: ENJOY YOUR SUCCESS OR LEARN FROM EXPERIENCE AND THEN MOVE ON

L ife presents us with a variety of experiences, and some are more fun than others. The final step in resolving a situation is to savor what went well, learn from what didn't, and then move on to the next adventure that awaits you. This chapter will give you some tips on how to do that.

ENJOY YOUR SUCCESS

How did things turn out? What did your evaluation show? Was your decision a good one? Are you satisfied? If so, hooray for you. You are a successful decision maker and should feel very proud of what you have accomplished. The good news is that success builds on success. As you keep honing your skills, future decisions will become even easier. You can't expect them to ever be easy, but practice does pay off.

Remember that for the purposes of this book, *a good decision is one with few surprises.* If you anticipated possible complications, took care of problems before they happened, and experienced an outcome that was suitable for you, you are a success.

Savor Your Achievement

Now it's time to give yourself some well-earned kudos. Do you make the time in your busy life to do that? Savoring success doesn't have to take long. Perhaps all you need to do is lean back in your chair and say, "Self, you did good. You worked hard, and things turned out okay. Not perfect, but much better than in the old days when you merely drifted or let other people tell you what to do." Smile and nod your head up and down. Try it right now. If someone happens to walk in the room and interrupt you, tell that person what happened and what you are doing. Otherwise, he or she will think you are talking to yourself, which of course you are!

It is very important to congratulate yourself. After all, who else is going to do it? In the long run, no one's opinion of you matters as much as your own. If you're like most people, you're very quick to beat up on yourself and dwell on your failures. Doing so can make you lose perspective on how your life is really going. You are entitled to spend at least the same amount of time congratulating yourself on your successes. Do it now!

Reward Yourself

Positive rewards are very motivating. Put them into your life as part of your hour of joy program. Fill each day with small satisfactions; they lead to contentment.

What can you do to reward yourself? Can you take a break? Have a cookie? Call a friend? Walk around the park? If your decision is a big one, why not throw yourself a party? What a wonderful way to share your success. Besides, you can do it your way. I am very big on having parties for oneself. No one else can read your mind about what you want as well as you can.

Surround Yourself with Success

Make it easy to remind yourself of things that turned out well for you. A file cabinet is no place for a letter of commendation. You want it out where you can see it and savor the memory of a wonderful day when things went well. Surrounding yourself with fond memories is fun and doesn't take much money.

> *Tip*
> *Surrounding yourself with fancy cars, clothes, and stereos that you didn't pay cash for is not success. It is debt. Don't confuse the two.*

Three things you can do to surround yourself with success are to create a

1. *Success wall.* Hang up everything that makes you feel good. For example, you can post a letter from a supplier awarding a major contract that you worked hard to get, certificates of completion of classes, or pictures of a dedication. Anything is okay if it reminds you of what a good thinker you are and what you have experienced.

2. *Success notebook.* Take a three-ring notebook and put tabs in it for the various parts of your life or job. Then insert positive memories in each section. Not only do these reminders make you feel good, they document your progress through the path of life. Also, for people who have to sell themselves or a product, this notebook is essential to remind you that your slow days don't last forever and the phone will ring again.

3. *Success folder.* At a minimum take one of your blank project folders, label it "Recognition," and file in one place the records of your accomplishments. Then, when the bad decision days hit, pull it out and comfort yourself.

LEARN FROM EXPERIENCE

How did things turn out? Not so well. You say you feel like an idiot, embarrassed yourself beyond all recognition, feel pain so bad that you could—and in fact did—cry? Did you lose? Get beat? Miss by one point? Get rejected? Get turned down? What else can you add to the list of woe?

Sorry to hear about your troubles, but if it's any comfort, you are not alone. Failure, disappointment, and loss happen to everyone. Welcome to the world of humanity. The difference is in how people respond. I read recently that hypochondriacs aren't any sicker than the rest of us; they just don't realize that it's normal to hurt, ache, and get colds. The way around both hypochondria and bad decisions is perspective.

Your goal is to learn what you can and then bounce back from adversity. There are two parts to that: dealing with your attitude and dealing with your behavior. One recommendation right now is to face reality. If things have not gone well, be the first to admit it. Just as some people can't acknowledge their successes, people at the other extreme can't acknowledge their failures. Denying that something hasn't gone well doesn't impress anyone; it just makes you appear to be out of touch with reality.

Attitude Checks

You have a choice about how you feel about your decisions. Here are some tips to help you gain perspective on days of disappointment.

Be realistic about life; it's hard for everyone. Expect but don't dwell on pain and disappointment. They're part of life and provide a counterpoint to the highs. A life that is nothing but highs is flat. Go for the roller coaster of ups and downs; it's more exciting. Not only that, no one has it easy or thinks he or she does.

Lu was riding the subway and overheard a young woman talking to her mother in loud, anguished tones about how the checks from her first bank account had come back with her telephone number misprinted. Lu was astonished to realize that this woman was in agony over what was objectively a very trivial issue. Lu told me she never forgot that all of us decide for ourselves what is hard. Perception is everything.

Tip
Discard painful reminders that drag you down emotionally. For example, after you have learned what you can, feel free to give to charity a gift that was really an insult, file forever a report that was poorly received, or tear up a party photo that is embarrassing. In other words, don't set yourself up to be reminded over and over once the lesson has been learned. Let it go.

Seek perspective. Most rejection, loss, and pain aren't personal. Most likely, nobody is out to get you. The world out there is a big place with a lot of smart people, and the reality is that you can't win them all. Humbling as it is to accept, you're probably not as important in the grand scheme of things as you think you are. Life goes on, and so will you.

Remember that *lost pride is a small price to pay for an interesting life.* If you keep mourning the results of yesterday's decisions and what didn't turn out right, all but other sad mourners will avoid you. Don't let that happen to you. Being hung up on the past is a recipe for bitterness and regret.

Putting things into perspective is *not* rationalizing or making excuses. Avoid people who make you feel bad and make fun of you as you struggle to learn and grow. They probably are threatened by your determination and courage. If it's family members, don't go home or confront them. Say, "I am trying very hard to work through this, and your support, not negative remarks, would be appreciated and much more helpful." If it's friends, get new ones. You've probably outgrown them.

> *Tip*
> *Grieve safely. Working through a heartbreaking outcome may require that you fully acknowledge your pain and wallow in it for a period of time. That is healthy and has to be done. But when the situation is a professional one, don't set yourself up by confiding in people who don't have your best interest at heart.*
>
> *For example, if you are struggling to balance a budget, think twice before telling a competitive counterpart. Otherwise you may find yourself off the next task force because "you're not good at numbers." Confide in a personal friend or coworker with whom you don't compete.*

Forgive yourself and others. After a reasonable length of time, unhook from resentment and pain. Otherwise you will be holding back your growth.

> *Tip*
> *Here is a simple, silly technique that you may find helpful. Do this when you are alone lest your coworkers think you are going crazy. While sitting at your desk, pretend your sad event has material- ized into the form of a little gremlin who is sitting on your left shoulder. Now turn your head and blow hard. As he, she, or it tumbles away in the breeze, so does your pain. The giggle that burbles out of you as you feel ridiculous is a form of healing.*

Remember that a loss of self-confidence is tempering and temporary.   Only you can work through your disappointments. Other people can comfort and encourage you, but they can't rebuild your faith in yourself. Tempering is the process of strengthening steel by putting it through fire. Your bad decisions and disappointments are tempering you. You are becoming stronger and less likely to break the next time. Also, remember the temporary nature of pain. I guarantee you that if you face reality, learn, and move on, your confidence will return stronger and deeper. This will take some time, but it will happen. Ask most widows and widowers; year 2 is easier than year 1. Time heals.

Set your emotions aside temporarily.   Sometimes you have to be very disciplined and rise to the occasion. Your mind becomes as strong as steel and as focused as a laser beam as you concentrate on coping with the situation at hand. I adopted this philosophy after hearing Tom Wenninger, former president of the National Speakers Association, say that as soon as he left his office to make a speech, the thought in his mind was "There is no such thing as a problem." This powerful mind-set enabled me to cope with dead microphones, burned-out light bulbs, and broken zippers with a smile and a shrug. There are times when you deal with the situa- tion and don't think about yourself.

CHAPTER TWELVE

Behavior

In addition to checking your attitudes, here are four steps you can take to get you through the pain of bad decisions.

Step 1: Openly admit your mistakes, errors, and poor results. My observation as a supervisor for over 20 years is that very few people can do this and that those who can go on to be very successful. Most people either become defensive or go into denial. Either behavior is not productive.

How do you admit mistakes? Simple. Prepare and practice a simple declarative sentence with two parts. Part 1 is a statement of the problem; part 2 shifts the attention forward. For example, if your report was criticized, you might say, "Yes, I'm disappointed the draft had to be reworked, but Mary gave me some terrific ideas for how to improve it. I can hardly wait to get started." If you don't define yourself as unduly beaten down, you won't be the topic of lunchroom conversations for very long.

Step 2: Fix the problem. A problem is a situation that in your judgment has a negative connotation. You want to convert a problem to a neutral situation with a solution. The fewer problems your name is associated with, the better. But problems do happen, and when they do, it's time to be a professional and exert extra effort. Pitch in and work overtime or on the weekend if that's what it takes to get things back on track. Draft, beg, or borrow extra support to help get the job done. Problems are part of life. Success means you fix them.

What if you can't fix the problem? Time for that backup plan you earlier outlined. If that doesn't work, you need to change direction, accommodating the change in plans.

Step 3: Apologize when necessary. When you are wrong, admit it promptly in the form of an apology. Don't grovel. Just be a responsible adult and admit that you made a mistake, you regret it, and you are sorry. It's very important to apologize. First, you'll like yourself better. A genuine apology is a great form of healing.

On a less noble note, you'll reduce the risk that someone will be out to get you later. Make friends, not enemies.

Step 4: Try, try, try again. Most people quit too soon. Pundits over and over remind us that the key to success is just plain not giving up. Life is full of second chances. You just have to take them. Taking second chances becomes easier when your mind shifts from the thought of what didn't happen in the past to what might happen the next time. Enter into a game of strategy with yourself; try a new approach or a revised plan.

Try is a powerful word that means "to attempt." When used literally (not as a passive-aggressive form of *No* or *I don't want to*), trying is value-neutral, a state in which you suspend judgment. You set aside the concept of winning or losing and instead enter the wonderfully curious position of waiting to see how things will turn out. Will you like this? Will you be successful? What will you learn? Only time will tell. Trying gives you permission to have some attempts succeed and some attempts fail. This mind-set is a powerful position, one that makes disappointments and failures part of life.

When is it time to quit trying? Perhaps when you've tried everything you can think of, when a win doesn't seem as important as it once did, when someone better qualified than you appears on the scene, or when the decision is final and you lost.

MOVE ON

Life presents an endless cascade of new situations to resolve. Yes, you close one door, but then you promptly open another as you move along your remaining days. The best way to move on is to be mentally prepared for closure. Nothing—even success—lasts forever. The second way is to have new projects that you can hardly wait to begin. That way, success is put into perspective and disappointments become part of the stream of daily activity so that you don't feel hopeless or permanently discouraged.

CHAPTER TWELVE

When you see change coming, a project ending, or your options narrowing, review your project folders and move the next one to the top of the pile. You may have time to work on it soon. If you haven't already, take some fresh file folders and create new labels such as "Fun Things to Do Someday" and "Things to Learn." Toss in articles, brochures, and business cards. Keep a steady stream of possibilities flowing into your life.

> *Remember*
> You have the rest of your life ahead of you. What are *you* going to do?

13 AFTERWORD

---

fter you stop procrastinating and master the techniques in this book, prepare for your life to change in ways you never anticipated. If you have followed the systems and tips, your life *will* be different a year from now. As your possibilities increase, so will your pleasure and joy. Opportunity awaits; all you have to do is quit procrastinating so that you bring closure to the past, resolve issues as they arise, and move into the future with eagerness and anticipation.

First, expect to have even more choices to make. For one thing, without that cloud of procrastination, guilt, and uncertainty hanging over you, you will have increased time and mental energy. That in itself will open doors. In addition, once you finally bring closure to all those "shoulds" you've been meaning to get around to, you may find entirely new interests and parts of your personality popping out. Take a minute and dream: What have you always wanted to try? The time is coming.

Second, you will increasingly be asked what you think and find that people are interested in your reply. Take the questions seriously and answer thoughtfully. People want to know. Prepare to be asked to serve on more task forces, committees, and special projects. Are you a manger, supervisor, or team leader yet? Such increased responsibility (and money) is certainly an option for good decision makers and nonprocrastinators. Maybe it's time to revise your career goals upward.

Third, prepare to become a role model for others. Your coworkers, direct reports, and team members will see how effective you are and, whether or not you are aware of it, imitate you. Share your techniques freely. Be patient and encouraging when you observe others procrastinating and struggling with difficult decisions. People are not born knowing how to be good decision makers. Remember that your children, nieces, nephews, and other impressionable young ones are watching you. Show them how to face difficult tasks and get them done and how to make choices without regrets. Remember that person who was a special influence on you? It's your turn now.

Prepare to receive reward and recognition, and prepare to receive it graciously, for you've earned it. When people tell you what a good job you are doing, thank them with a smile and a nod of acceptance. Savor those moments as a reward for a difficult job well done. Then, of course, bring yourself back to earth and get back to the tasks at hand. After all, you have a job to do and a future to face. The past is nice, but it's over.

Finally, prepare to have an impact on our society. As a thinker, nonprocrastinator, and good decision maker, you are one who will make the world a better place. Your department, company, and country need you and your ideas. Your suggestions, insights, and proposals will solve problems. Your family will be a functional, satisfying unit. You are one of those people who will make a difference in how the world turns. What an honor and responsibility. And why shouldn't it go to you? You deserve it!

THE PROCRASTINATOR'S GUIDE TO SUCCESS MIND-SETS

Do you know what to do? Yes or no?

If the answer is yes, then you are procrastinating because you know what to do and aren't doing it. Your challenge is to become a nonprocrastinator.

Remember:

You always have a choice, and that choice is to do something or do nothing.

Doing nothing is one of the most powerful choices you can make.

Do things right and you will have fewer things to do over.

Decisions are the building blocks of your life, and your mind is your most valuable decision-making tool.

Focus on the hour of joy you will create once your task is done.

Once you master procrastination, you will find that it is a nonissue.

Success is self-validating. Acknowledge and savor your successes.

Do the important tasks first, for that is where the payoff is.

Avoid busywork and low-return items.

Take a fresh approach to an old job.

Procrastination is all in your head. Projects aren't "hard"; they're "interesting."

Seek new mind-sets. Define yourself and your tasks differently.

Success means entering the Risk Zone. Things might go wrong or go right.

> If you are stuck, use your BEGIN-er's Checklist (Chapter 5) to figure out why.
>
> Lost pride is a small price to pay for an interesting life.
>
> Face your worst-case scenario and then assess what is likely to happen.
>
> Estimate the odds for success and failure.
>
> Push yourself; courage comes from within.
>
> You get a second chance. Have the courage to take it.

If your answer is no, you don't know what to do, then you are not a procrastinator. You are a thinker with situations to resolve. The two conditions are different; don't confuse them.

> **Remember and use the RESOLVE It! system:**
>
> **R:** Resolve something!
>
> **E:** Examine what you already know
>
> **S:** Step into the future
>
> **O:** Overcome the subtle factors
>
> **L:** Leap, lurch, or launch into action
>
> **V:** View and evaluate your results
>
> **E:** Enjoy your success or learn from experience and then move on

When you find yourself stuck, review the following list to jump-start your thinking process.

> Decision making begins when you become aware that a situation is changing.
>
> Decision making is a skill that improves with practice and good technique.
>
> A good decision is one with few surprises

Information is the raw material of your decisions.

Bring mental order to your chaos by doing a sort (Chapter 7)

Turn your gut-wrenchers into projects complete with folders.

Start with one thing and resolve that.

Know when to mull and when to judge.

To visualize success, look forward in time one to three years.

Go beyond the obvious in your thinking.

Use due diligence checklists (Chapter 9) to uncover subtle factors within and beyond your control.

You can always win if you never risk failure.

If all choices are equally appealing or unappealing, flip a coin; it doesn't matter.

The reason to evaluate your decisions is to do better the next time.

Admit your mistakes, lick your wounds, and move on.

Enjoy your success; you've earned it.

To repeat, lost pride is a small price to pay for an interesting life.

Do something. Seek new adventures.

Seek to grow and learn every day.

INDEX

INDEX

INDEX

About the Author

Lynn Lively is a popular speaker and writer on procrastination, workplace decision making, and clear-thinking skills, and is the author of *Managing Information Overload*. She is also the cofounder of American Pioneer Sonars, a company founded in 1981 and recognized by the Small Business Administration and former President Bush for excellence in exporting. Lynn welcomes your e-mail comments at LLIVELY@aol.com.